Iran's Role in Western Origins

Ronald C. Smith

Abstract

The purpose of this qualitative case study was to explore how a select sample of college-level history textbooks position Iran and Iranians in the origins of Western Civilization. Western Civilization history marginalizes, misrepresents, misappropriates, and/or omits Iran's positioning (Kincheloe, 2004; Daryaee, 2005; Anvarinejad, 2007; Daragahi, 2010; Ahkami, 2014; Vahdati, 2014). Further, the mainstream approach to teaching Western Civilization history includes the Judeo-Christian-Greco-Roman narrative. The researcher used a multi-faceted theoretical approach—decolonization, critical pedagogy, and Western Civilization History dilemma—since this study transcended historical revisionism. This collective case study involved eleven Western Civilization history textbooks that, according to the College Board's College-Level Examination Program (CLEP), are most popular among American college faculty. The researcher reviewed and collected expert opinion on the following five themes: (1) terminology and definition of Iran, Iranians, and Iranian languages; (2) roots and origins of Iranian peoples; (3) which Iranian peoples are noted in general; (4) which Iranian peoples in ancient Europe are specifically noted; and (5) Iranians in connection with six unique Western Civilization attributes. The researcher selected experts specializing in Iranian, Western Civilization, and Indo-European studies in formulating a consensus on each theme. The researcher then compared expert opinion to content in surveyed textbooks. This study found that the surveyed textbooks overwhelmingly omitted, ill-defined, misrepresented, or marginalized Iran and Iranians in the origins of Western Civilization.

TABLE OF CONTENTS

LIST OF FIGURES x

CHAPTER 1: INTRODUCTION 1

    Background and Context.. 3

    Statement of the Problem 5

    Purpose of the Study 6

    Research Questions 6

    Conceptual Framework 6

    Assumptions and Delimitations 7

    The Researcher... 8

    Significance of the Study 9

    Definitions of Terms 10

    Conclusion 12

CHAPTER 2: REVIEW OF THE LITERATURE 13

    Conceptual Thinking in the 21st Century 15

    Culture, Identity, and Root... 16

    Current Presentation of Iranian Studies in American Textbooks 18

        Bias, Orientalism, and Decolonization 18

        Marginalization, Misrepresentation, and Misappropriation..................... 20

        Omission 21

    Critical Pedagogy 23

    The Status of Western Civilization History and Iran's Position in

        Teaching of It 26

    Conceptual Framework 27

        Decolonization Theory 29

        Critical Pedagogy Theory 30

        Western Civilization History Dilemma Framework 30

    Conclusion 31

CHAPTER 3: METHODOLOGY 34

    Rationale for Qualitative Research Design 35

    Rationale for Case Study Methodology 35

    Research Sample 36

    Overview of Information Needed 37

    Data Collection 38

    Data Analysis 41

    Ethical Considerations and Trustworthiness 43

    Strengths and Limitations 43

CHAPTER 4: RESULTS 45

    Analysis Method 45

    Presentation of Results 50

    Theme 1— Terminology and Definition of Iran, Iranians, and Iranian languages 50

        Definition of Iran 50

        Definition of Iranians 52

        Definition of Iranian languages 54

Theme 2—Roots and Origins of Iranian Peoples 55

    Proto-Indo-Iranians, Airyanam Vaejo, and the Iranian Plateau 56

Themes 3 and 4— Coverage of Iranian Peoples 58

    Selected Iranian inhabitants of Asia 58

    Selected Iranian inhabitants of Europe 60

Theme 5— Iranians in Connection with Six Unique Western

    Civilization Attributes 61

    Greek Philosophy as a Unique Western Trait 61

    Law and Order as a Unique Western Trait 66

    Human Rights as a Unique Western Trait 73

    Democracy as a Unique Western Trait 77

    Individualism as a Unique Western Trait 79

    Christianity as a Unique Western Trait 81

Discrepancies during Data Collection 90

Summary 90

CHAPTER 5: CONCLUSION 96

Interpretation of Findings 97

Implications 102

Recommendations for Action 104

Recommendations for Further Study 106

Conclusion 109

CHAPTER 1

INTRODUCTION

The study of the *historical DNA* of a place, including Europe, involves learning about all the different peoples who have settled in the area throughout the ages (Cole & Symes, 2017, p. 196). Cole and Symes (2017) claimed since this is not an easy task, one should focus on influences and interactions rather than identities (p. 196). This study explored how history textbooks position Iran and Iranians in the origins of Western Civilization. Here, the researcher uses Persia and Iran interchangeably even though Persia is one of many nations of Iranian stock (see Definition of Terms).

Based on the literature review, Western Civilization history marginalizes, misrepresents, misappropriates, and/or omits Iran's positioning (Kincheloe, 2004; Daryaee, 2005; Anvarinejad, 2007; Daragahi, 2010; Ahkami, 2014; Vahdati, 2014). The researcher did not discover any contrary opinion. The Father of American English dictionary and education and a creator of early American culture Noah Webster said, "the original seat of the German and English nations was Persia" (p. ix), and "[t]he ancestors of the Germans and English migrated from Persia" (p. 4). According to an 1857 edition of *Emerson's United States Magazine* (later *Putnam's Magazine*), Persia and countries east of the Caspian Sea, who were of the same stock, gave birth to Hindus of India and "the formidable nations of Goths, Vandals, Franks, and Saxons, who established new kingdoms on the ruins of the Roman Empire" (p. 259).

German philosopher G. W. F. Hegel (1837/1956) wrote,

> Asia separates itself into two parts—Hither and Farther…the nations of Hither Asia…are related to the West…. The Persians are the first Historical People; Persia was the first Empire that passed away…. The principle of development begins with the history of Persia. This therefore constitutes strictly the beginning of World-History. (pp. 173-174)

According to Columbia University professor of Indo-European languages A. V. W. Jackson (1899), followers of a contemporary of Socrates, Sophist Prodicus, "are reported to have boasted their possession of secret writings of Zoroaster [ancient Iranian reformist and philosopher]; and even a Magian [Iranian Zoroastrian sage] teacher, one Gobryas, is claimed as instructor of Socrates" (p. 8). Author and translator of Ukrainian literature Florence Livesay (1918) noted,

> The man of the stone age in the Ukraine left very few clues to his mode of life…. But it is plain that from Asia, from Ariastan (Iran), another race followed, who heaped their grave-hills upon the graves of the primeval inhabitants. Undoubtedly the Antes were a tribe of that great Iranian invasion. Ariastan not only begot Ukrainians and all European nations, but it was the cradle of Persians and Hindus as well. (p. 114)

French philosopher and scholar Henry Corbin (1978) remarked, "For Persia, the old Iran, is not only a nation or an empire, it is an entire spiritual universe, a hearth and meeting place in the history of religions" (as cited in Cheetham, 2009, p. 2). Farrokh (2015) cited Spatari's (2002) claim that as early as 500-450 BCE, there are indications of Iranian presence in Calabria, Southern Italy (p. 75).

The purpose of this case study was to explore how history textbooks place Iran and Iranians in the origins of Western Civilization. History is about meaning-making and learning about the ancestors. Historians should review history holistically to find a more meaningful and continuous paradigm (Mohammad, 2013). In conceptualizing the role of the marginalized, historians return justice to disenfranchised groups while providing meaningful information in Western studies. The researcher used qualitative case study methodology to evaluate eleven college Western Civilization history textbooks. The publication dates of the textbooks fell between 2000 and 2017. The researcher purposefully selected these textbooks based on popular use among college faculty, according to the College Board's College-Level Examination Program (CLEP).

This chapter begins with an overview of the background and context that frames the study. Following this is the statement of the problem, the purpose of the study, and research questions. This chapter also includes the conceptual framework, assumptions and delimitations, the researcher's background, and the study's significance. The chapter concludes with definitions of key terms.

Background and Context

This study covered undergraduate level survey courses on the history of Western Civilization. Specifically, the researcher focused on the Age of Antiquity that falls under History of Western Civilization I course (HIS101) at a community college in Virginia (see Appendix A). The purpose of HIS101 is to survey the general history of the Western world from about 3000 BCE to 1600 CE especially the social, intellectual, cultural, and religious attributes. The course objectives include explaining the changing geopolitical structures of the Western world, defining key individuals in Western Civilization, identifying social forces at work in the evolution of early Western history, and describing significant cultural achievements of ancient Western Civilization. Finally, HIS101 course topics include studying the origins of human societies in the

West including ancient Near East, classical Greece, the Romans, Byzantine Empire, and Eastern Europe (see Appendix A).

In studying world civilizations, the American Historical Association (AHA) listed four great civilizations—the Chinese, the Indians, the Greeks, and the Mayans—as a major theme in studying the Age of Antiquity (Smith, 2013, p. 1). This is contradictory to the concept of the first world empire, the Achaemenid Persian Empire (550-330 BCE) (Brosius, 2006, p. 1; Wiesehöfer, 2006, p. 1; Dandamaev & Lukonin, 1989, p. 367). Shajari (2015) stated that the Persian Empire is considered by some experts as the largest of all time in managing some 44% of the then world population (49 million of the 112 million) (p. 26). Contact by ancient Greeks with the Persian Empire triggered the formation of a Hellenic identity (Brosius, 2006, p. 3). This empire also served as a model for later empires such as the Hellenistic kingdoms, the Roman Empire, and the Byzantine Empire (Dandamaev & Lukonin, 1989, p. 367; Malraux, 1945/1964, p. 188). Sissa (2012) suggested that, based on ancient Greek historian Herodotus, the invention of democracy took place among the 6th c. BCE Persian aristocrats debating forms of government, some 15 years prior to political reforms by Cleisthenes leading to a democracy in Athens (p. 261).

In Dr. Kaveh Farrokh's views, the academia often marginalized Iranian influences from the ancient world (as cited in Ahkami, 2014). Historian Howard Zinn's claim is the best expression of the urgency of this problem. He explained that the serious way in which history deceives people is through omissions (as cited in Kreisler, 2010, p. 358). Under ethic of critique, Gay (2013) suggested educators conduct their own research and analysis of mainstream educational materials and examine various ethnic descriptions and interpretations of events. Educators should use their own research and insight to reconstruct or replace deficient content in mainstream materials to transform critical cultural consciousness. Textbook and Academic

Authors Association (2009) encouraged textbook authors to provide current, competent, balanced, and accurate information in their publications (p. 1). In accordance with transformative leadership educational practices (Shields, 2010), this study looked at how current history textbooks place Iran and Iranians in the origins of Western Civilization.

Statement of the Problem

Mohammad (2013) claimed the justification for studying history is to understand the totality of human experiences through factual analysis and approach the discipline holistically. Iran's coverage in the history of Western Civilization is not a mature topic. Some studies group Iranians under a regional classification such as the Middle East, merge them with a macro group such as Muslims, or combine them with non-Iranians such as Arabs (Kincheloe, 2004; Morgan and Walker, 2008; Goldschmidt Jr. & Davidson, 2010; Salameh, 2011).

Critical pedagogy is important in transformational leadership in education. This study follows Salinas, Blevins, and Sullivan's (2012) view on critical historical thinking in that not only should historians examine the past through primary sources but include the marginalized or omitted histories—controversial histories—so that formation of an identity is more meaningful (pp. 19-20). Bruno-Jofré and Schiralli (2002) named content knowledge and mastery of the subject matter as part of critical pedagogy for history educators (p. 121), and claimed teaching history should not rest on ulterior political goals (p. 123). Finally, given the current debates about replacing Western Civilization history as a limited perspective glorifying imperialism and colonialism with World history given its broader nature (Ricketts, Wood, Balch, & Throne, 2011), a thorough coverage of Iran in the origins of Western Civilization might address that curriculum dilemma.

Based on the literature review, Western Civilization history marginalizes, misrepresents, misappropriates, and/or omits Iran's positioning (Kincheloe, 2004; Daryaee, 2005; Anvarinejad, 2007; Daragahi, 2010; Ahkami, 2014; Vahdati, 2014). Iranians are Indo-Europeans and have inhabited Asia and Europe since the Age of Antiquity. Therefore, previous theories such as Orientalism and Eurocentrism (Dabashi, 2015; Daryaee, 2005; Shariati, 2010), nativism (Morgan, 2008), or bias against Middle Eastern peoples (Brockway, 2007) as noted in the literature review did not provide sufficient explanation as to the marginalization, misrepresentation (Anvarinejad, 2007; Foltz, 2016; KPFA, 2014; Morgan & Walker, 2008; Vahdati, 2014), and omission of (Bachrach, 1973; Daragahi, 2010; Kincheloe, 2004) Iran's positioning in the history of Western Civilization.

Purpose of the Study

The purpose of this qualitative case study was to discover how college history textbooks in a select sample position Iran and Iranians in the origins of Western Civilization.

Research Questions

This study focused on the following areas: Terminology and definition, roots and ancestry, and cultural characteristics. The study attempted to discover how Western Civilization textbooks define *Iran, Iranians*, and *Iranian languages;* explain the roots and origins of Iranians; cover Iranian peoples in the Age of Antiquity; teach about Iranian peoples in Europe during the Age of Antiquity; and discuss Iranian attributes in Europe during the Age of Antiquity.

Conceptual Framework

The focus of this study fell in line with the Zinn Education Project (2016) where the goal is to be more honest in looking at the past and delivering to the students a more accurate and holistic understanding of history rather than textbooks filled with random names and dates. As a form of revisionist history, historians may use the viewpoint of marginalized people in social history to reinterpret the historical record (Berube, 2002, p. 49). Revisionists look at sources more critically and advocate historical interpretations that are inclusive. However, sometimes revisionists may be politically motivated (Coohill, 2014, p. 3). The multi-faceted theoretical approach—decolonization, critical pedagogy, and Western Civilization History dilemma—was especially important since this study transcended historical revisionism. The approach in this study was to revise, not reinterpret.

Assumptions and Delimitations

As a history educator, the researcher made the following assumptions about this study. First, historians are supposed to tell the truth about what happened in the past. Dunn's (2013) suggestion underpinned this assumption asserting that as soon as a historian has another goal besides discovering and relaying what happened then a historical account is contaminated. Second, textbooks are key tools in higher education. Kornblith and Lasser (2005) and Jaschik (2005) reinforced this assumption in that textbooks reach a much wider audience and shape how college students encounter history. Many educators rely solely on textbooks to design class curriculum and lesson plans (Kornblith & Lasser, 2005). Therefore, content matters. Third, historians, well versed in the field, write and revise college history textbooks. Kornblith and Lasser's (2005) report supported this assumption in that authors, not editors or marketing personnel, control the content of textbooks although only a handful of publishers produce the majority of college textbooks.

Additionally, the Age of Antiquity is an important part of learning about the history of Western Civilization. The College Board's College-Level Examination Program (CLEP) provided the basis for this assumption by estimating that 38-44% of test materials in Western

Civilization I exams cover the Age of Antiquity including the Near East, the Greeks, and the Romans (College Board, 2016, p. 1). Students in Western Civilization I courses should demonstrate the ability to understand important factual knowledge about the origins of Western Civilization and distinguish between relevant and irrelevant materials (College Board, 2016).

A limitation in this study involved the college level that these history textbooks serve. The study focused on undergraduate survey courses on the history of Western Civilization. Since the curriculum of many undergraduate programs in America include liberal arts, students take history courses such as Western Civilization to meet general education course requirements or fulfill elective credits towards graduation (International Student, 2016). The one-semester class that includes the Age of Antiquity (3000 BCE to 5th c. CE) covers some 4500 years of history involving the development of the West spanning Asia, Europe, and parts of Africa. This study noted the limitations on information that fits in these compressed textbooks aimed at a wider student audience. Nawrotzki and Dougherty (2013) supported this limitation in claiming that survey history courses target non-majors and "introduce students to broad historical themes in an area" (p. 1). These survey classes usually have large class sizes and cover a wide range of materials in one semester. The educators often lack the time to practice historical methods or delve into subfields with the students (Nawrotzki & Dougherty, 2013).

The Researcher

At the time of conducting this study, the researcher was an adjunct faculty member in a History Department at a Virginia community college. She had been teaching the history of Western Civilization for six years. The researcher has a Masters of Arts in History specializing in ancient Iran, and has studied Iran in relation to the history of Western Civilization for over twelve years. She has been interviewing, publishing, and blogging regarding history for more than eight years. The researcher brought to the inquiry process practical experience and content knowledge as a history educator, researcher, and writer. Additionally, she had a fascination since childhood in finding common ground among historical peoples because of her mixed cultural background including Iranian (Persian) and Irish (Celtic). The researcher's passion was the driving force in formulating a meaningful and contributive study not only for herself but society-at-large. She recognized that these valuable and relevant experiences with respect to this study might also bring biases regarding research design and analysis. The researcher was committed to focusing on the purpose of the study and maintaining critical self-reflection through journaling and peer review.

Significance of the Study

In a 1901 edition of *American Education* magazine, one learns that in some New York schools the classroom decorations involved combining history and the arts to inspire the imagination. For example, starting with the Native American arts students moved to the Persian Period before the Greek Period whereby students learned Iranian heroic lessons of courage and truthfulness (Braman, 1901). Yet, in both HIS101 (Appendix A) and CLEP's (College Board, 2016) course descriptions, Persia (Iran) was not even listed as a separate entity. Students jumped from the Near East to the ancient Greeks and Romans when studying the Age of Antiquity.

The mainstream approach to teaching Western Civilization history includes the Judeo-Christian-Greco-Roman narrative (Parcel & Taylor, 2015; Arnn, 2014, p. 1; Le Gates, 2001, p. 19; p. 6; Papper, 1995, p. 131). This study explored how selected textbooks covered the positioning of Iran and Iranians in the origins of Western Civilization as opposed to expert opinion (see Appendix B). The study contributed to knowledge base and practical application (Bloomberg & Volpe, 2012, p. 66). Educators and students would note there is more to the origins of Western Civilization than a limited focus on Judeo-Christian-Greco-Roman heritage. This would be a significant shift in paradigm surrounding the development and identity of the West given how textbooks view and report on Iran. This study helped improve content of educational materials to address marginalization and omissions of Iran's positioning as noted in the literature review. Finally, the way in which textbooks present Iran in the origins of Western Civilization might address some of the arguments by critics favoring World History for a broader and more inclusive historical perspective.

According to Bowden (2012), the way in which people uncritically receive and perceive information is altered when something is revised. Historians should take into account new findings and perspectives to improve knowledge about history (Pavlac, 2010). Howard Zinn viewed the study of history as a way to find answers to current problems in recommending that history teachers bring up controversial questions and issue of equality while making sure not to replace one type of indoctrination for another (as cited in Miner, 1994). Hence, a fresh, holistic, and non-victimized point of view in addressing Iran's positioning in the origins of Western Civilization was timely, relevant, and contributive.

Definition of Terms

Age of Antiquity. The period between 3000 BCE and 5th century CE.

Indo-European. The name of a family of languages with marked similarities that evolved from a common source with a wide distribution from India to Ireland (Cole and Symes, 2017). The main groups under this family tree are Celtic, Germanic, Balto-Slavic, Italic, Anatolian, Indo-Iranian, Greek, Armenian, Albanian, Tocharian (Fortson, 2004).

Iran. The continuation of the ancient term *Aryan* possibly meaning noble or lord (Frye, 2004, pp. 2-3). Ancient sources referred to Iranian peoples such as the Persians and the Medes as

Aryans, and ancient Iranians "were conscious of their difference from the settled peoples [between the Ganges and Euphrates] over whom they came to rule" (Frye, 2004, pp. 2-3). Other examples of *Iran* as derivative of *Aryan* are as follows. Iranian king Darius the Great's 5th century BCE royal inscription at Naqsh-e Rustam (DNa) reads, "I am Darius the Great King, King of Kings,…an Achaemenian, a Persian, son of a Persian, an Aryan, having Aryan lineage" (Avesta Zoroastrian Archives, 2006, p. 28). Diakonoff (2003b) noted all Indo-Iranians from Scythia to India called themselves by the general name *Arya* (Aryan) (p. 37). Cook (2003) discussed how Iranians or Aryans wore trousers and turbans (p. 247). In one of the greatest medieval chronicles, *The Ecclesiastical History*, 12th c. English monk and historian Orderic Vitalis called the Irish by the same name as Iranians (as cited in O'Brien, 1898, p. 121). Further, O'Brien (1898) asserted both Ireland (*Eiran*) and Persia were called Iran (p. 122), and the Irish language is "the primitive Iranian or Persic language" (p. 126).

Iranians or Iranian peoples. Various peoples of Iranian stock lived across Europe and Asia since the Age of Antiquity. Some of them, in whole or in part, are as follows: Mede, Persian, Parthian, Saka, Scythian, Sogdian, Sarmatian, Alan, Bactrian, Kurd, Azari, Lur, Bakhtiari, Cimmerian, Hephthalite, Massagetae, Kambojas, Khorvat, Serboi, Jassic, Ossetian, Shirazi, Tajik, Phrygian [depicted in Iranic attire along with other Iranians wearing tunic, pants, and red felt hat known as the "Freedom cap"], Mitanni [Indo-Iranian], Saggarthian, Corduchi, Caspian, Arachosian, Khwarezmian, Dahae, Zarangian, Arimaspi, Pallava, Arian, Leucosyri, Rhoxolani, Iazyges, Siraces, Parni, and Ashvakas (Vasseghi, 2014, p. 3). This study focused on 27 Iranian tribes based on expert opinion (see Appendix C).

Origins. The birth or emergence of Europe's civilization during the Age of Antiquity.

Persia or Persian. Although Persians are one of many Iranian peoples, because of their historical significance and popularity, their name has become interchangeable with Iran or Iranians. All Persians are Iranians, but not all Iranians are Persians.

Position or positioning. Iran's place in socio-political development of Western Civilization such as early settlers in Europe during the Age of Antiquity.

Western Civilization. The history of European peoples (Cole and Symes, 2017).

Conclusion

This study contributed to an understanding of Iran's positioning with respect to the origins of Western Civilization. It fell in line with the Zinn Education Project (2016) where the goal is to be more honest in looking at the past and deliver to the students a more accurate and holistic understanding of history rather than textbooks filled with random names and dates. It also tackled the *so what* factor as far as the significance of Iran's positioning in the origins of Western Civilization. Chapter 2 is a foundational and current literature review in relation to the study. Chapter 3 describes the proposed design and methodology for the study including proposed data collection and analysis methods. Chapter 4 includes the results of the study. Chapter 5 discusses findings, recommendations, and conclusions. Appendix A includes History of Western Civilization I (HIS101) course content summary. Appendix B is a list of experts used in this study. Appendix C is a list of 27 Iranian tribes identified by expert opinion. Appendix D is a quick reference to summary of findings.

CHAPTER 2

REVIEW OF THE LITERATURE

Goldschmidt Jr. and Davidson (2010) claimed people tend to identify Middle East history with that of the Arabs and Muslims (p. 121). In studying world civilizations, the American Historical Association (AHA) listed four great civilizations—the Chinese, the Indians, the Greeks, and the Mayans—as a major theme in studying the Age of Antiquity (Smith, 2013, p. 1). This is contradictory to the concept of the first world empire, the Achaemenid Persian Empire (550-330 BCE) (Brosius, 2006, p. 1; Wiesehöfer, 2006, p. 1; Dandamaev & Lukonin, 1989, p. 367). Shajari (2015) stated that the Persian Empire is considered by some experts as the largest of all time in managing some 44% of the world population at that time (49 million of the 112 million) (p. 26). Contact by ancient Greeks with the Persian Empire triggered the formation of a Hellenic identity (Brosius, 2006, p. 3). This empire also served as a model for later empires such as the Hellenistic kingdoms, the Roman Empire, and the Byzantine Empire (Dandamaev & Lukonin, 1989, p. 367; Malraux, 1945/1964, p. 188).

In Dr. Kaveh Farrokh's views, the academia often marginalized Iranian influences from the ancient world (as cited in Ahkami, 2014). Historian Howard Zinn's claim is the best expression of the urgency of this problem. He explained that the serious way in how history deceives people "is not that lies are told, but that things are omitted. If a lie is told, you can check up on it. If something is omitted, you have no way of knowing it has been omitted" (as cited in Kreisler, 2010, p. 358). This literature review aligned the following multiple perspectives as objectives to determine Iran's positioning in the history of Western Civilization: (1) the relevancy of conceptual thinking in the 21st century; (2) the meaning of identity, culture, and roots; (3) the current presentation of Iranian studies in American textbooks; (4) critical pedagogy; and (5) the status of Western Civilization history and Iran's position in teaching of it.

Conceptual thinking breaks through disjointed narratives about the Western Civilization as observed by the French art theorist and Minister of Cultural Affairs Andre Malraux, "There is no Europe. There never was…. There has been a vaguely European culture…Europe is that which is not Asia" (Malraux, 1945/1964, 184). In order to evaluate Iran's role, the researcher explored the concepts of identity, culture, and roots with respect to studying Western Civilization history. Once the researcher discussed these perspectives then she examined the actual presentation of Iranian studies in the history of Western Civilization to explore gaps in the field. Pro-world history advocates are challenging the relevancy of teaching Western Civilization (Ricketts et al., 2011). Although Western cultures should know more about the world, people should learn about their own background as much as possible in order to understand other cultures and origins. Therefore, Iran's role might play a part in the debate about the status Western Civilization history.

The researcher used searching parameters such as Iranian history and Persian history in American textbooks, Iran's coverage in textbooks, Middle East portrayal in textbooks, conceptual thinking, critical pedagogy, decolonizing indigenous and marginalized peoples, and the status of Western Civilization history. The selection criteria involved publications within the past ten years with the exception of sources on historical content, which may be older given the content and saturation in the field. The research based credibility of the sources on the following considerations: where was the source published, who wrote it, and was the source timely and appropriate to the field (Columbia College, 2016). The researcher looked for articles, blogs, scholarly studies, dissertations, interviews, and books. The researcher evaluated the references for scholarly value and relevancy as well as historical accuracy.

Conceptual Thinking in 21st Century

Franzese (2014) advocated a need for a "more right-brain integrative, empathic, nonlinear and intuitive" (p. 8) way of discerning and organizing information. Conceptual skills or out-of-the-box thinking is one of the main 21st century traits. Those with conceptual skills make connections across disciplines in gaining a deeper understanding of ideas which utilizes analysis, synthesis, reasoning, critical thinking, and creativity (Starfire Education, 2016). Conceptual thinking paves the way for pattern finding. It is a required skill in order to see the big picture when discerning Iran's role in a developing Western Civilization. Conceptual thinking shows that the apparently unrelated cultures create *cohesive wholes* that in turn transform a possibly incoherent Western Civilization curriculum (Ricketts et al., 2011, p. 19) into a viable, uniting part of a larger world history.

Wheatley's (2006) work provides a lens to look at a developing Western Civilization holistically and in a new light despite the limited Judeo-Christian-Greco-Roman narrative (Parcel & Taylor, 2015; Arnn, 2014, p. 1; Le Gates, 2001, p. 19; p. 6; Papper, 1995, p. 131). Wheatley (2006) challenged the current Newtonian way of looking at phenomena and conducting scientific research. That is, with the rise of quantum physics showing that reality is based on observation and relationships are key determinants in terms of probabilities rather than predictions, researchers should look at things as a whole rather than in parts. A historian's main challenge is in line with Wheatley's (2006) claim that to understand the whole of history after years of studying historical content in fragments, one must conceptualize or discern the unseen connections of what might appear to be separate entities. Since meaning and purpose are two key elements in humanity, historians should connect the dots between shared ancestry and cultural heritage. Wheatley (2006) stated people achieve self-knowledge through their need for identity, desire for new information, and forming relationships.

Conceptual thinking is part of having a fresh look at Iran's positioning in the history of Western Civilization. Historians should review the history of Western Civilization holistically to find a more meaningful and continuous paradigm. In conceptualizing Iran's role in the history of Western Civilization, historians return justice to a marginalized people, provide meaningful information in Western studies, and tackle the sense of disconnect and fragmentation in history of Western Civilization.

Culture, Identity, and Roots

History is about meaning-making and learning about the ancestors. British historian Corfield (2008) argued that studying history is "essential for 'rooting' people in time" (p. 1). Those who are rootless often live rootless lives hurting themselves and others in the process. Corfield (2008) warned that educators should find new ways to teach the subject in an interesting manner so that it is not too fragmented. Therefore, history should be taught "more formally, more systematically, more accurately, more critically and more longitudinally" (Corfield, 2008, p. 6).

> A definition of culture is a collection of commonly held cognitions that are held with some *emotional investment* [emphasis in original] and integrated into a logical system or cognitive map that contains cognitions about *descriptions, operations, prescriptions,* and *causes* [emphasis in original]. They are *habitually used* [emphasis in original] and influence prescription, thinking, feeling, and acting. (as cited in Argyris, 2010, p. 146)

Culture supports a sense of order and predictability in the world. It helps answer questions about what exists, what should be done, how it should be done, and why things are done in a particular way (Argyris, 2010). Northouse (2013) defined culture "as the learned beliefs, values, rules, norms, symbols, and traditions that are common to a group of people" (p. 384).

Bruner (2008) claimed that between the two ways in which the mind works–computational and culturalism–it is culture that plays a role in forming of a distinctly human mind. That is, processing information is not sufficient for meaning-making since human civilization, which is what one studies in the field of history, rests heavily on symbolism. Therefore, culturalism, which is how the mind depends on shared symbols or culture for its existence, is the way by which people create and communicate meanings and may interpret texts from a part in relation to the whole. Given Bruner (2008) viewed education as part of a whole culture, not a stand-alone, then historians should educate the public with as much accuracy as possible regarding origins and connections between and among cultures.

Wheatley (2006) noted that a strong identity allows self-reference "to create greater stability and autonomy" (p. 85) because we can make better decisions when facing changes by knowing who we are and what our purpose is. A clear sense of identity in individuals as well as organizations is the only way to remain independent from the environment. Identity involves a "lens of values, traditions, history, dreams, experience, competencies, [and] culture" (Wheatley, 2006, p. 86). In order for a system to become healthier, it needs to know more about itself. Wheatley (2006) helped entities develop greater self-knowledge by connecting people to the fundamental identity of the community, new information, and others anywhere in the system despite traditional boundaries. Meaning is discerned when we realize that change is meaningful to us (Wheatley, 2006).

In history, terminology is important when improper, inadequate, or missing definitions of peoples affects our understanding of ancestry and cultural connections. With respect to research on indigenous people, "terminology can represent something more than just a word. It can represent certain colonial histories and power dynamics" (The University of British Columbia, 2009, p. 1). In terminology, a loaded word can divide, misrepresent, and control a people's identity. Therefore, the best way to avoid being disrespectful to a people is to provide the most specific definition for a population (The University of British Columbia, 2009).

Historians should trace cultural and ancestral connections between Iran and the Western nations for Iran to be meaningful to Western peoples. This includes proper and sufficient definitions. Meaning must change for people for Iran's positioning in the history of Western Civilization to change. Therefore, historians must provide accurate terminology and highlight the importance of roots, culture, and identity.

Current Presentation of Iranian Studies in American Textbooks

Iran's coverage in the history of Western Civilization is not a mature topic. Some sources deal with Iran in the study of Western Civilization directly or treat it as part of a larger grouping or regional coverage such as the Middle East.

Bias, Orientalism, and Decolonization

Brockway's (2007) mixed methods study revealed a biased perspective of the Middle East in ten secondary school textbooks via terminology, data omissions, and inaccurate information. Given Mainstream Media's negative portrayal of Arabs and Islam, textbooks do not sufficiently counter this bias by providing accurate and comprehensive information to avoid stereotyping and misconceptions about the Middle East. In lumping Iran with the Middle East as a whole, Iran's position in the history of Western Civilization is not properly covered given Iran is not an Arab nation and Islam is not native to Iran. In a globalization and leadership study in which researchers divided 62 nations into ten distinct clusters based on common language, religion, geography, and history, Iran was listed under the *Southern Asia* cluster, not the *Middle East* (Northouse, 2013, p. 390). Therefore, lumping Iran in the Middle East with respect to the history of Western Civilization is inaccurate.

Daryaee (2005) claimed the coverage of Iranian history in textbooks is either non-existent or often skewed and biased based on Eurocentric tendencies, colonialism approaches, or Orientalism views. Daryaee (2005) suggested that the academia's views on Iran should be decolonized. To reclaim Iran's heritage and historiography, Shariati (2010) opposed Eurocentrics' attempts to de-nationalize and de-culturalize Iran. Shariati (2010) was concerned with the level of manipulation against Iranian history and national identity. This is important because national identities and national consciousness are major pillars in social, economic, and political formations of a people. Shariati (2010) described the attribution of Iranian contributions to non-Iranians as painful since the act denied Iranians their rightful place in historical context. Dabashi (2015) covered the modern Western fascination with and use of all things Persian as a step beyond Orientalism. His goal was to override the East-West divide to de-alienate and disabuse the postcolonial site so that it is not second to the West. In advocating decolonization, Smith (2012) claimed research should be *talked back to* as it is part of global imperialism (p. 226). That is, through underlying codes and rules those in power use research to regulate scientific paradigms and ideological constructions and representations in promoting imperialism and colonialism. According to Smith (2012), talking back to mainstream institutions to recover and decolonize a people involved rewriting and re-righting the position of indigenous peoples in history.

Marginalization, Misrepresentation, and Misappropriation

Anvarinejad (2007) reviewed nine major textbooks in California to see how Iran's history is taught in textbooks, took surveys from experts in the field of Iranian studies to note important topics that should be taught, and conducted a literature review to identify important elements in Iranian history. Anvarinejad (2007) concluded that California State Standards and world history textbooks did not make any significant references to Iranian history.

Vahdati's (2014) interview also focused on how California history textbooks taught virtually nothing about the Persian Empire except the notion that the Persians are enemies of Greek civilization. In an interview, history professor John Lee claimed he was surprised at how California textbooks reflect the outdated, one-sided ancient Greek perceptions of ancient Persia, which is contradictory to current scholarship in the field (as cited in KPFA, 2014). Lee noted that current history standards with respect to how Iran's is covered in California textbooks are misleading or incomplete. Further, popular culture based on movies perpetuated stereotyping of Iranian peoples and is not reflective of their historical role. These films are highly biased towards the ancient Iranian civilization (as cited in KPFA, 2014). Lee believed proper teaching of Iranian history in textbooks is significant to show that the world has always been interconnected, and teaches critical thinking so students may learn to look at different narratives in history. Lee advocated unraveling these distortions of Iranian history in textbooks reflecting 19th century European imperialism (as cited in KPFA, 2014).

Morgan (2008) suggested that *nativism*—the belief that only those of Northern and Western European ancestry may be American and world leaders—might have influenced how 20th century textbooks covered the Middle East. Morgan (2008) found bias towards Islam, the Arab political system, the impact of colonialism, and the daily life of Middle Easterners. Morgan and Walker (2008) cited how previous studies showed that Middle Eastern peoples are "marginalized, stereotyped, or omitted in school textbooks" (p. 86). Foltz (2016) noted the misrepresentation of medieval Iranian scholars, who transmitted the classical *Western* culture to Medieval Europeans, as Arabs, and that Western media is often biased and negative towards Iranian culture.

Omission

Bachrach (1973) pursued his study—an important monograph cited by Halfond (2015)—because the academia ignored the role of Iranian Sarmatians and Alans tribes in the conquest of and settlement in Europe. Daragahi (2010) reported that examination of American textbooks reveals that there is virtually nothing about Iran. Even the index at the back of the textbooks does not list any relevant terms with respect to Iran. Cohen (2011) referred to how academia ignores Persian poetry, one of Iran's greatest cultural contributions. Kincheloe (2004) tackled modern misrepresentations and omissions regarding Iran's history in American education system as well as the media's distortions on the subject matter. He claimed most Americans know very little about Iran, confuse Iranians with Arabs, and do not know that Persia and Iran are the same. Sources and Mainstream textbooks provided inaccurate information by omitting historical context about Iran. Stausberg (2008) warned that the study of Zoroastrianism is very delicate as one of the most under-researched areas despite a global rise of Neo-Zoroastrianism since the 1979 Islamic Revolution in Iran. Experts generally view Zoroastrianism as a contributing influence on other religions such as Judaism and Christianity (Stausberg, 2008, p. 562), the very elements that are in mainstream approach to teaching Western Civilization history.

Some of the sources reporting on Iran's coverage in Western Civilization history textbooks claimed that Iran is confused with Arabs or Islam (Kincheloe, 2004; Anvarinejad,

2007; Foltz, 2016). This adds to the problem of Iran's marginalization in that it keeps Iran colonized under a foreign identity (Arab) and a religious belief of non-Iranian origin (Islam). Not only do sources omit or ignore Iranians and their position with respect to a developing West, but they also unjustly and grossly misrepresent Iranian peoples' historical identity.

Some studies placed Arabs and Islam in the center stage leaving out non-Arabs such as the Turks and the Iranians as well as many other religions in Western Asia (i.e., Middle East) (Brockway, 2007; Morgan, 2008; Morgan & Walker, 2008). Those handling studies on behalf of this region either do not know or understand the history and identity of Iran. This is misleading and assumes that improper coverage of Iran's position in the history of Western Civilization falls under nativism. Many who criticize textbooks in treating Middle East as if its only inhabitants are Arabs and Muslims commit the same unjust acts when the focus of their study is Arabs, Arab contributions, or Islam.

The literature review regarding Iran's positioning in the history of Western Civilization was based on the following lenses: bias, Orientalism, decolonization, marginalization, misrepresentation, misappropriation, and omission. The multidimensional approach here was necessary because the sources view the problem from one or more of those perspectives. There was no single dominating point of view that explained Iran's current positioning in the history of Western Civilization. Therefore, a collective approach provided the most comprehensive image of what was happening in the field.

Critical Pedagogy

Kincheloe (2008) discussed the politics of knowledge and the control of data by the elite and transnational corporations. Science, media, and standardized educational systems use of misleading information help those in power to achieve their economic and political goals. Kincheloe (2008) regarded critical pedagogy as a force that may bring transformative changes by (1) uncovering old and new knowledges to change our relationship with the world and others while building a new way of emancipation from what we learn from our past and present, (2) discovering how those in power control knowledge, (3) asking out-of-the-box questions to understand that reality is not what it seems, and (4) having passion for equity and challenging value-free knowledge. Kincheloe (2008) supported practicing critical pedagogy in teaching Western Civilization history and writing about Iran's positioning in its teaching to invalidate an *Us v. Them* view with respect to historical connections between peoples and decolonizing a marginalized group.

Samiei (2014) noted with respect to Greco-Persian history, "the current discourse has continued to rely heavily on a number of thematic topoi, which, broadly speaking, suggest that the freedom loving European Greeks were in the fight of their lives against the despot-worshipping, prostrate-junkie hordes of Asiatic Persians" (Samiei, 2014, p. 244). He asserted one might present Persian/Iranian history in a better fashion. That is, an important academic field with relevance to Iranian studies is "the modern and multifaceted discipline of Indo-European studies" (Samiei, 2014, p. 246).

Salameh (2011) discussed the influence of donations by some Middle Eastern despots to distinguished American academia for the purpose of gaining favor in pre-determined outcomes and tainting the advancement of knowledge in academic institutions by prejudicing their mission.

Salameh (2011) specifically criticized and rebuffed recent moves by the academic institutions to change the name of the historical Persian Gulf to Arabian Gulf, and warned against dire consequences if academia indulged such ideological falsities for political gains. Salameh (2011) suggested that many of these shady Middle Eastern donors are part of a system that practices cultural suppression and historical revisionism detrimental to the history of the various inhabitants of the region. He claimed both the West and Islam engaged in colonialism and imperialism. He rejected the labeling of the region as the *Arab world* given the Middle East is anything but exclusively Arab. Salameh (2011) asserted the label *Arab world* is misleading since non-Arabs in the region such as Iranians and Turks resisted Arabization for centuries. He warned that political relations between the West and the Arabs have resulted in ignoring historical clarity and academic decency. Salameh (2011) stated that the academia ignores the historical multiculturalism and diversity in the Middle East and instead anoints everyone there as *Arabs* in legitimizing this erroneous monolithic view of the Middle East.

Shapiro and Gross (2013) defined the ethic of critique as challenging the status quo, deconstructing the consensus, addressing inequities, and asking difficult questions. It is connected to critical pedagogy by "encourage[ing] educators to not only be aware of injustices but to take action to transform the practices and structures that perpetuate them" (New York University, 2016, p. 1). Gay (2013) noted that the problem with textbooks and educational materials is that often their coverage of ethnic and cultural diversity is distorted and incomplete (p. 58). Under ethic of critique, Gay (2013) encouraged educators to "critique teaching resources and strategies, and compensate for inadequacies when necessary" (p. 59). Gay (2013) suggested educators conduct their own research and analysis of mainstream educational materials and examine various ethnic descriptions and interpretations of events. Educators should use their own research and insight to reconstruct or replace deficient content in mainstream materials to transform critical cultural consciousness.

Shapiro and Gross (2013) stated that ethic of critique which is characteristic of critical theory and critical pedagogy causes awakening to injustices and inequities especially in education. In that sense, Smith (2012) discussed decolonization of marginalized peoples such as indigenous groups especially with respect to how historians write history since history is about justice and power. Therefore, an important part of decolonizing marginalized people is to revisit how and who writes history. Those who are at a disadvantage may resist injustice and inequity in historical portrayals by telling their version of the past and claiming their history.

According to the American Historical Association, historians should be involved in critical dialogue and respect the integrity of historical records. They should ensure that sources do not alter, suppress, or change evidence (American Historical Association, 2011, p. 3). They should present different perspectives about historical events since "absolute historical knowledge is denied us" (American Historical Association, 2011, p. 5). Historians should acknowledge personal biases affecting, and financial support from special interest groups influencing, scholarly work. Good teaching involves accuracy and rigor in transmitting information. Textbooks and teaching materials should include "the diversity of human experience, recognizing that historical accuracy requires attention both to individual and cultural similarities and differences and to the larger global and historical context within which societies have evolved" (American Historical Association, 2011, p. 9).

Educational leaders should promote transparency, integrity, fairness, trust, and learning as well as protect responsibility, equity, and justice (National Policy Board for Educational Administration, 2015, p. 10). With respect to curriculum and instructional materials, educational leaders should pursue effective pedagogy and teach what is intellectually challenging (National Policy Board for Educational Administration, 2015, p. 10). Finally, textbook authors should provide current, competent, balanced, and accurate information in their publications (Textbook and Academic Authors Association, 2009, p. 1).

Critical pedagogy is important in transformational leadership in education. If there are errors or problems in mainstream content then an educator has an obligation to address those issues. History educators should be even more sensitive to a people's history and contributions.

The Status of Western Civilization History and Iran's Position in the Teaching of It

After examining official catalogues of 75 American colleges and universities representing all 50 states, Ricketts, Wood, Balch, and Throne (2011) claimed the history of Western Civilization is disappearing from the undergraduate curriculum in American colleges (North, 2015; Kiley, 2011; London, 2011). Instead, in support of multiculturalism, world history is rapidly replacing it as well as American history. Ricketts et al. (2011) advocated teaching both courses and especially Western Civilization, because it provides Americans with knowledge about the roots of their civilization, its contribution to globalization, and its role in transforming human condition. Here, one can see the importance of learning about origins and roots as Corfield (2008) encouraged.

Ricketts et al. (2011) noted that this trend is due to a larger pattern of curricular disintegration in that teaching Western Civilization "had come to be seen as a form of apologetics for racism, imperialism, sexism, and colonialism. Demoting it from a requirement or eliminating it altogether, could therefore be viewed as a blow against these oppressions" (Ricketts, et al., 2011, pp. 14-15). It appears that in perceiving that something is missing from or fragmented in Western Civilization content, educational institutions are now marginalizing and omitting it from their curriculum in America, a Western nation. The idea of offering Western Civilization as a history course is now a dilemma.

The status of the history of Western Civilization as a subject matter was relevant given pro-World history advocates claimed that Western Civilization is lacking or insufficient. A concern was its treatment of other cultures. If historians properly cover Iran's role, then they might address the Western Civilization history dilemma.

Conceptual Framework

The researcher had a fascination since childhood in finding common ground among historical peoples because of her mixed cultural background including Iranian (Persian) and Irish (Celtic). Henstrand (2015) claimed language is an important tool in understanding cultures, and that cultures encompass "the values and traditions that are known to all members of the society" (p. 29). The researcher strived to understand the patterns of connection among these languages and cultures especially since mainstream textbooks and institutions often omit or skew their ancestral relationships.

The researcher's passion was the driving force in formulating a meaningful and contributive study not only for herself but society-at-large. The research first started with the desire to understand and learn more about ancient Iranians, their beliefs, and their way of life since these were lacking in mainstream contents. In time, the researcher observed various patterns in omissions, misrepresentations, misconceptions, and marginalization with respect to Iranian peoples and their place in the history of Western Civilization. The purpose of the study was to decolonize a people and return a part of history that was missing in the teaching Western Civilization in American colleges.

The three-part theoretical framework found in the literature review that supported this study were decolonization, critical pedagogy, and Western Civilization History dilemma. As cited in Jaime (2008), decolonization theories refer to "reclaiming power through sovereignty, self-determination, self-identification, and self-education" (p. 2). Jaime (2008) claimed that the academia views stories, identity, and culture as told by the colonized peoples as invalid and illegitimate resources for knowledge. Therefore, when the colonized defined itself then the decolonization process began. Decolonization is "a long-term process involving the bureaucratic, cultural, linguistic, and psychological divesting of colonial power" (Smith, 2012, p. 101). The colonized peoples should revisit history as an important part of the decolonization process, because there is unfinished business of approaches to the past. Smith (2012) claimed getting to know the past "has been part of the critical pedagogy of decolonization" (p. 36), and to know another side of history is to have other knowledge. In teaching the history of the West, mainstream textbooks treat Iran with insignificance, irrelevancy, or dismissiveness. This study decolonized Iran and Iranians by focusing on the origins of Western Civilization. Iran's place in the description and definition of the origins of the West was the most significant gap in the field. It transcended other gaps such as exploring Iran's contributions to Western arts and sciences, social, political, and symbolic realms, as well as Iran's colonization by Islam.

According to Breuing (2011), there was no universal definition for critical pedagogy, but elements of critical pedagogy include critical reflection and action, involvement of the outside world and transformation, and highlighting activism (p. 11). The definitions and goals of critical pedagogy most suitable to this study included social consciousness, social change, examining hidden assumptions to work toward justice, multicultural education, emancipation, promotion of critical thinking, empowerment, transformation, and profound learning experience (Brueing,

2011, pp. 8-9, 11). Conceptual thinking and critical pedagogy were required in discussing the importance of identity, culture, and roots in the field of history. By marginalizing or omitting Iran's positioning within the curriculum, educators taught a fragmented view of the origins of Western Civilization. This placed the legacy and heritage of Iranians in danger, while Westerners learned an incomplete perspective of their own history.

World history refers to macro-history or transregional, transnational, and transcultural history. World history involves comparative history or the big picture of cultural interchange (The World History Association, 2015). In addressing challenging historical experiences in the history of the West such as colonialism, imperialism, and racism as well as concerns with multiculturalism, the academia is marginalizing and removing Western Civilization history as a subject in favor of world history (Ricketts, et al., 2011). The focus of this study on Iran's place in the origins of Western Civilization addressed parts of the academic dilemma and supported the purpose of the course by tackling deficient content.

Decolonization Theory

Historian Kaveh Farrokh stated academia often marginalized Iranian influences from the ancient world (as cited in Ahkami, 2014). Daragahi (2010) described how the examination of American textbooks reveals there is virtually nothing about Iran. Stausberg (2008) warned that the study of Zoroastrianism is one of the most under-researched areas despite being one of the oldest religions with enduring influences and impact on other religions. Cohen (2011) cited how academia ignores Persian poetry, one of Iran's greatest cultural contributions. Daryaee (2005) claimed that textbooks hardly cover Iranian history, and if in any capacity, they show a skewed and biased portrayal, and suggested that academia's views on Iran need to be decolonized. Smith (2012) provided guidance on decolonizing peoples in teaching history.

Critical Pedagogy Theory

According to Mohammad (2013), the justification for studying history is to understand the totality of human experiences through factual analysis and approaching the discipline of history holistically. Wheatley (2006) discussed the new science of looking at problems holistically. Kincheloe's (2004) focus was on the current economic agenda influencing and shaping American understanding of modern Iran via media's educational power misrepresenting the ancient people as a terrorist nation and religious fanaticism outside the historical context. Kincheloe (2004) underlined the continued miseducation of the American public by news sources, and encouraged teachers to play a transformative role in correcting these misconceptions.

Western Civilization History Dilemma Framework

The history of Western Civilization as a subject is being debated (Ricketts, et al., 2011; North, 2015; Kiley, 2011; London, 2011). This dilemma arises from multiculturalism considerations and content that is deemed lacking or weak leading to a sense of marginalization and oppression. Recalling Malraux's (1945/1964) claim that Europe is what is not Asia, it follows that perhaps Iran's positioning in the history of Western Civilization would address this long-standing gap.

The focus of this study—understanding the positioning of Iran and Iranians in the origins of Western Civilization—fell in line with the Zinn Education Project (2016) where the goal is to be more honest in looking at the past and delivering to the students a more accurate and holistic understanding of history rather than textbooks filled with random names and dates. Anfara and Mertz (2015) explained that a theory is useful when it "tells an enlightening story about some phenomenon" (p. 5). Mutch (2015) added that framing deals with how meaning is put together and who controls what. Anfara and Mertz (2015) preferred to view theory as a person's profound, unique, and fresh perception of reality or a phenomenon. They noted that in social science research such as history, researchers draw on theories from various disciplines, because these different perspectives can enhance a study.

The multi-faceted theoretical approach—decolonization, critical pedagogy, and Western Civilization History dilemma—was especially important since this study transcended historical revisionism. The approach in this study was to revise, not reinterpret. According to Bowden (2012), the way in which people uncritically receive and perceive is altered when something is revised. Historians should take into account new findings and perspectives to improve knowledge about history (Pavlac, 2010). In studying history, Howard Zinn viewed it to find answers to current problems in recommending that history teachers bring up controversial questions and perspectives on equality while making sure not to replace one type of indoctrination for another (as cited in Miner, 1994). Hence, a fresh, holistic, and non-victimized point of view in addressing Iran's positioning in the origins of Western Civilization was timely, relevant, and contributive.

Conclusion

This literature review aligned the following multiple perspectives as objectives: (1) the relevancy of conceptual thinking in the 21st century; (2) the meaning of identity, culture, and roots; (3) the current presentation of Iranian studies in American textbooks; (4) critical pedagogy; and (5) the status of Western Civilization history and Iran's position in teaching of it. Figure 1 shows how this study drew upon the fields of quantum physics (study of the whole rather than parts; interconnectedness), transformative leadership (deep and equitable change;

deconstruction and reconstruction of social knowledge, emancipation and equity, and moral courage) (Shields, 2010), sociology (culture and terminology), anthropology (ancestral links), and psychology (decolonization and identity). The study rested on the theories of decolonization, critical pedagogy, and Western Civilization History dilemma.

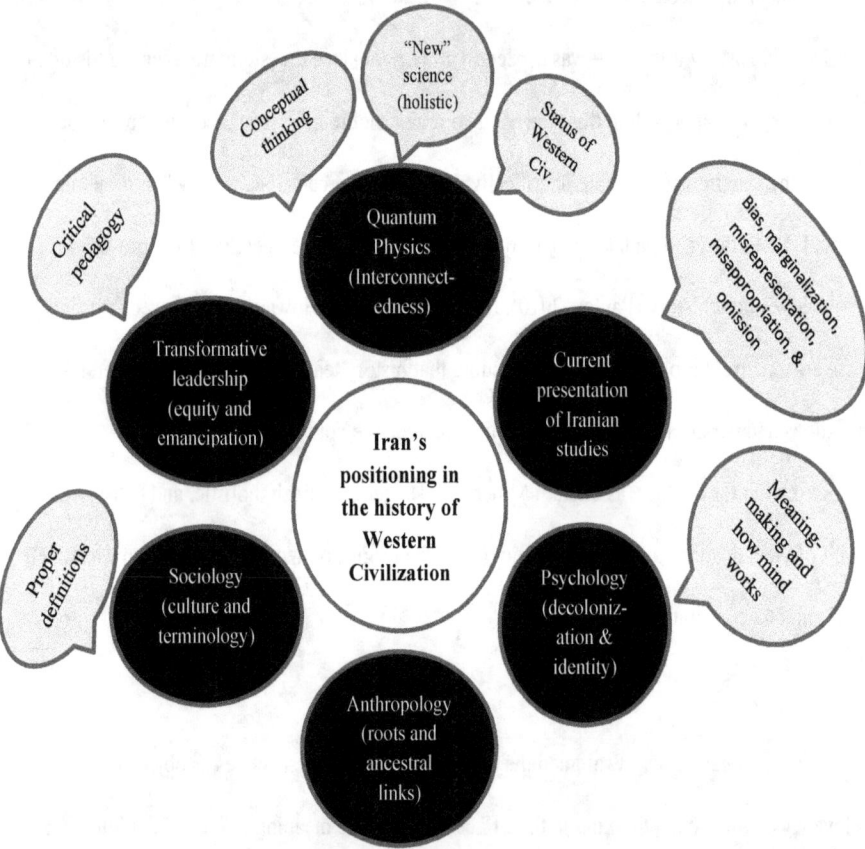

Figure 1. Concept Mapping. This figure illustrates the thematic approach in conducting a literature review regarding Iran's positioning in the history of Western Civilization.

Conceptual thinking helped in looking at history holistically rather than fragmented narratives and a collection of unrelated events. In order for Iran's history to matter to the West, the literature review explored the concepts of identity, culture, and roots. The core of the literature review was to explore sources on the presentation of Iran in Western Civilization history. The review also discussed the idea of critical pedagogy in relation to the responsibilities of a transformative historian and educator. Finally, the review presented the recent debate about the viability of teaching Western Civilization history and how Iran's positioning might possibly affect this dilemma.

Understanding how Iran's position in the history of Western Civilization is taught fell in line with the Zinn Education Project (2016) where the goal is to be more honest in looking at the past and delivering to the students a more accurate and holistic understanding of history rather than textbooks filled with random names and dates. The literature review illuminated Iran's marginalization and omission in textbooks covering the history of Western Civilization. Further, the perspectives or solutions offered in some of the sources were limited, weak, and improper. In some cases, the references added other problems by continuing the misrepresentation or mischaracterization of Iran and its heritage due to a lack of clear and comprehensive knowledge of Iran. Thus, a fresh, holistic, and non-blaming point of view in addressing Iran's positioning in the history of Western Civilization was timely, relevant, and contributive. Based on the literature review, the most important gap in the field or the *so what* factor was Iran's positioning in the origins of Western Civilization.

CHAPTER 3

METHODOLOGY

The purpose of this qualitative case study was to explore how history textbooks in a selected sample place Iran and Iranians in the origins of Western Civilization. Iranians inhabited Asia and Europe since the Age of Antiquity. They are also an Indo-European people. Therefore, previous theories such as Orientalism and Eurocentrism (Dabashi, 2015; Daryaee, 2005; Shariati, 2010), nativism (Morgan, 2008), or bias against Middle Eastern peoples (Brockway, 2007) as noted in the literature review did not provide sufficient explanation as to the marginalization, misrepresentation (Anvarinejad, 2007; Foltz, 2016; KPFA, 2014; Morgan & Walker, 2008; Vahdati, 2014), and omission of (Bachrach, 1973; Daragahi, 2010; Kincheloe, 2004) Iran's positioning in the history of Western Civilization. In seeking to understand this phenomenon, the researcher focused on the position of Iran and Iranians in the origins of Western Civilization. The study attempted to discover how Western Civilization textbooks define *Iran, Iranians,* and *Iranian* languages; explain the roots and origins of Iranians; cover Iranian peoples in the Age of Antiquity; teach about Iranian peoples in Europe during the Age of Antiquity; and discuss Iranians in connection with unique Western Civilization attributes.

This chapter describes the study's research methodology and includes discussions around the following areas: (a) rationale for qualitative research design, (b) rationale for case study methodology, (c) description of the research sample, (d) overview of information needed, (e) methods of data collection, (f) analysis and synthesis of data, (g) ethical considerations and trustworthiness, and (h) strengths and limitations.

Rationale for Qualitative Research Design

One of the goals of science is to collect objective and accurate data about a problem (Drew, Hardman, & Hosp, 2008, p. 74). The primary purpose of qualitative research is to understand a phenomenon in a meaning-making effort without testing or proving a theory for cause-and-effect. The researcher functions as a primary instrument in collecting data (Merriam, 2009, pp. 14-15). Researchers may conduct a qualitative study when there is a need to explore an issue, empower people, and formulate theories (Creswell, 2013, pp. 47-48). Qualitative research describes how people interpret what they experience (Merriam, 2009) or, in this study, how textbooks present the positioning of Iran and Iranians in the origins of Western Civilization.

Rationale for Case Study Methodology

Within the framework of a qualitative approach, this study was most suited for a case study design. As a strategy of inquiry or a methodology, case study explores contemporary multiple bounded systems over time using in-depth data collection involving documents (Creswell, 2013, p. 97). With respect to gathering data, case study is very flexible (University of Surrey, 2016). This collective case study involved Western Civilization history textbooks published between 2000 and 2017 that are most popular among American college faculty according to the College Board's College-Level Examination Program (CLEP). By collecting data from eleven most popular textbooks, the researcher derived an in-depth understanding of the problem. This case study was heuristic because it provided a discovery of new meaning and/or confirmed what the literature review described about Iran's positioning in the origins of Western Civilization history (Merriam, 2009, p. 44). A case study was suitable here because the problem was in the field of education and the methodology allowed the researcher to investigate complex social units consisting of multiple variables (Merriam, 2009, p. 50).

Research Sample

Merriam (2009) stated one of the most common forms of non-probabilistic sampling type is purposeful sampling or "selecting *information-rich* cases [emphasis added]" (p. 77). Creswell (2013) noted that typical sampling reflects the normal or average (p. 158). Although Creswell (2013) recommends four or five case studies for collecting sufficient data to identify themes and conduct cross-case theme analysis (p. 157), the researcher used eleven textbooks. The researcher selected the following textbooks based on CLEP's recent survey identifying the most popular Western Civilization history textbooks among American college faculty (College Board, 2016). CLEP listed thirteen textbooks on studying Western Civilization history. The researcher obtained the following nine from that CLEP list based on availability through either her employer's textbook vendors (electronic versions) or history department textbook supplies (in print versions):

- Cole, J., & Symes, C. (2017). *Western Civilizations: Their history and their culture*. New York, NY: W. W. Norton & Company, Inc. (electronic version) (updated edition to CLEP's Coffin and Stacey, *Western Civilizations, Brief Edition* (W. W. Norton));

- Hunt, L., Martin, T. R., Rosenwein, B. H., & Smith, B. G. (2017). *The making of the West: Peoples and cultures*. Boston, MA: Bedford/St. Martin's (electronic version);

- Kidner, F. L., Bucur, M., Mathisen, R., McKee, S., & Weeks, T. R. (2014). *Making Europe: the story of the West*. Boston, MA: Wadsworth (electronic version);

- King, M. L. (2000). *Western civilization: A social and cultural history*. Upper Saddle River, NJ: Prentice Hall (in print version);

- Kishlansky, M., Geary, P., & O'Brien, P. (2010). *Civilization in the West*. Upper Saddle River, NJ: Pearson (in print version);

- McKay, J. P., Hill, B. D., Buckler, J., Crowston, C. H., Wiesner-Hanks, M. E., & Perry, J. (2014). *A history of Western society.* Boston, MA: Bedford/St. Martin's (electronic version);

- Noble, T. F. X., Strauss, B., Osheim, D. J., Neuschel, K. B., Accampo, E. A., Roberts, D. D., & Cohen, W. B. (2011). *Western civilization: Beyond boundaries*. Boston, MA: Wadsworth (electronic version);

- Sherman, D., & Salisbury, J. (2014). *The West in the world: A history of Western civilization*. New York, NY: The McGraw-Hill Companies, Inc. (electronic version); and

- Spielvogel, J. J. (2015). *Western civilization*. Stamford, CT: Cengage Learning (electronic version).

The researcher also included the following textbooks that were not part of the CLEP list given they were also readily available through her employer's textbook vendors:

- Campbell, K. L. (2015). *Western Civilization: A global and comparative approach, Volume I: To 1715*. New York, NY: Routledge (electronic version), and

- Perry, M., Chase, M., Jacob, J. R., Jacob, M. C., Daly, J. W., & Von Laue, T. H. (2016). *Western civilization: Ideas, politics, and society*. Boston, MA: Cengage Learning (electronic version).

Overview of Information Needed

A study has value when it informs and improves practice (Creswell, 2013, p. 255). The researcher focused on five themes with respect to the positioning of Iran and Iranians in the origins of Western Civilization: (1) terminology and definitions of *Iran, Iranians,* and *Iranian languages*, (2) roots and origins of Iranian peoples, (3) which Iranian peoples are noted in general, (4) which Iranian peoples in ancient Europe are specifically noted, and (5) Iranians in connection with unique Western Civilization attributes. With respect to the fifth theme—unique Western Civilization attributes—the researcher focused on classical legacy such as Greek philosophy, the rule of law such as protection of human rights, democracy, individualism, and Christianity (Huntington, 1996; Duchesne, 2011).

The researcher selected these five themes based on the study's focus on terminology and definition, roots and ancestry, and cultural characteristics. The researcher chose these themes based on her expertise in the field. In order to discover how history textbooks position Iran and Iranians in the origins of Western Civilization, one should search the content for terminology and definition, roots and ancestry, and cultural characteristics. In this study, the collective expert opinion on each theme provided the control measures by which the researcher reviewed the content of the selected history textbooks.

In order to choose experts in accordance with the thematic approach, the researcher assumed the role of a textbook author. That is, if she were to write a textbook on Western Civilization history without omitting or marginalizing the positioning of Iran and Iranians then she would consult a diverse group of experts specializing in Iranian, Western Civilization, and Indo-European studies in order to formulate a consensus on each topic. The researcher provided a full list of experts in Appendix B. The researcher then reviewed the eleven college-level Western Civilization history textbooks and recorded verbatim by page number what they reported on the five themes.

Data Collection

Words provide data in qualitative research (Merriam, 2009, p. 85). Additionally, relevant and authentic documents may be located in providing "descriptive information, verify emerging hypotheses, advance new categories…offer historical understanding, track change and development" (Merriam, 2009, p. 155). The data collection was extensive, drawing from eleven textbooks as well as comparing findings with what experts said regarding the key themes. The researcher set up five files for each theme and within each sub-file(s) collected what experts said about the theme, as applicable, versus what each of the eleven textbooks stated about the theme. The researcher was the primary instrument and kept journal entries to track thoughts while collecting data.

The files were set up as follows:

File 1 – Theme 1

    A) Definition of *Iran*

        a. Definition by experts

        b. Recorded verbatim and by page number what textbooks stated

    B) Definition of *Iranians*

        a. Definition by experts

        b. Recorded verbatim and by page number what textbooks stated

    C) Definition of *Iranian Languages*

        a. Definition by experts

        b. Recorded verbatim and by page number what textbooks stated

File 2 – Theme 2

    A) Roots and origins of Iranians

        a. Expert opinion on the matter

        b. Recorded verbatim and by page number what textbooks stated

File 3 – Theme 3

The researcher made a list of known Iranian peoples according to Vasseghi (2014) and checked expert opinion to develop a list of Iranian tribes that majority of experts designated as Iranian (see Appendix C). These experts designated the tribes as Iranian, Indo-Iranian, Iranian-speaker, or of Iranian country.

File 4 – Theme 4

This was a subsection of Theme 3. The researcher isolated European Iranians from Waldman and Mason (2006) and reviewed expert opinion to select the ones that majority of experts designated as Iranian inhabitants of Europe (see Appendix C). The researcher noted the following information for each tribe in each textbook: did the textbook mention the tribe, did it mention origins, and in what context did it discuss the tribe.

File 5 – Theme 5

The researcher noted expert opinion on positioning of Iran and Iranians for the following unique characteristics of Western Civilization (Huntington, 1996; Duchesne, 2011), and reviewed each of the eleven textbooks to see what they each explained in that regard verbatim and by page number.

A) Greek philosophy

B) Law and order

C) Human rights

D) Democracy

E) Individualism

F) Christianity

Data Analysis

The purpose of this qualitative case study was to explore how history textbooks placed Iran and Iranians in the origins of Western Civilization. The researcher collected data from eleven textbooks most commonly used by college faculty to teach the history of Western Civilization, according to CLEP. The purpose of data analysis was to answer research inquiries and might be the only part based on personal preference (Merriam, 2009, p. 176). The researcher used an inductive approach since earlier theories cited in the literature review failed to explain what was happening (Mack, Woodsong, MacQueen, Guest, & Namey, 2005). An inductive approach in qualitative studies allowed the researcher to work through the data from the *bottom up* so that she could develop patterns and themes by putting data "into increasingly more abstract units of information" (Creswell, 2013, p. 45). That is, the researcher worked back and forth between the database and themes in formulating a comprehensive set of themes (Creswell, 2013, p. 45).

Content analysis can help "develop an understanding of the meaning of communication" (Elo & Kyngäs, 2008, p. 108). Authors write textbooks as written communications that convey information about a subject matter to the educators and the students. In this study, the researcher explored what was happening in the content of selected textbooks in relation to the positioning of Iran and Iranians in the origins of Western Civilization. Content analysis focuses on meanings and consequences. The researcher may use this method in qualitative or quantitative research as well as in an inductive or deductive way. Besides the three steps of preparation, organizing, and reporting, content analysis has no other systematic rules (Elo & Kyngäs, 2008, p. 109).

Following Creswell's (2013) recommended techniques for a case study, the researcher created and organized files for the data, read the data for content analysis, and coded the data.

The researcher used categorical aggregation to establish patterns. Through direct interpretation of data collected verbatim, the researcher developed naturalistic generalizations of what she learned from the case study. The researcher presented the data using narrative and tables (Creswell, 2013, pp. 190-191). The researcher followed a sequential content analysis to assess the nature of the data (Merriam, 2009, pp. 152-153). The researcher treated each selected textbook as a comprehensive case and then compared different textbooks in a cross-case analysis format (Merriam, 2009, p. 204).

The researcher made a table for each theme to compare what experts said versus what the eleven Western Civilization history textbooks presented verbatim. The researcher placed data collected for each theme from subject textbooks under the following columns: proper coverage, misrepresented/misappropriated, inaccurate/incomplete, skewed/biased, or marginalized/omitted. The researcher noted her perspectives or data organizational approaches might change or formulate after data collection with emerging categories or themes.

The reporting of data verbatim from eleven college textbooks most commonly used by faculty in teaching Western Civilization established the credibility of the study (Trochim, 2006). With respect to transferability of the results in this qualitative study, the researcher may apply the findings to other aspects of Iranian positioning in Western Civilization history such as the Middle Ages or the Modern Era (Trochim, 2006). Other researchers may readily repeat the study since expert opinions and the eleven history textbooks are publicly available (Trochim, 2006). The researcher used expert opinions as basis for the eleven textbook content analysis. The researcher recorded data collected from the textbooks verbatim and by page number. This secured confirmability of the study (Trochim, 2006).

Ethical Considerations and Trustworthiness

Ethical issues for this study fell under analyzing and reporting data (Creswell, 2013, p. 59). The researcher reviewed eleven textbooks for validity purposes. To avoid disclosing only positive information and results, Creswell (2013) advised to report contrary findings and honestly (p. 59). Drew, Hardman, and Hosp (2008) reminded researchers "[a]ny breach of integrity during the development, execution, or dissemination of results, whether it be intentional or unintentional, will seriously weaken or even invalidate a research study" (p. 78). Creswell (2013) stressed the importance of validation or "an attempt to assess the 'accuracy' of the findings, as best described by the researcher and the participants" in a study (pp. 249-50).

Strengths and Limitations

Case studies are limited to the integrity and sensitivity of the researcher. That is, a researcher may select from the data almost anything that can illustrate what she or he aims to portray (Merriam, 2009, p. 52). The researcher discussed potential biases in the study. More than any other methodology, case studies may lead to confirming preconceived notions (Merriam, 2009, Table 3.1, p. 53). Additional limitations in cases studies involve the concepts of reliability, validity, and generalization (Merriam, 2009).

The researcher maintained a journal throughout the phases of the study in order to reflect on the data collected. The researcher also chose to approach the study from a broad perspective before focusing on specific elements to minimize bias. For example, the researcher collected data on as many Iranian tribes as covered by the surveyed textbooks before focusing on those tribes that were ancient inhabitants of Europe. Further, the researcher collected data on multiple unique characteristics of Western Civilization to keep a broader perspective. The researcher believed these steps provided more opportunities to find relevant data in the history textbooks.

Since this case study involved reviewing surveyed textbooks for content, then the value of the data depended on whether it was relevant to the research questions and the researcher acquired the information in a practical way (Merriam, 2009, p. 153). In this study, textbook documentary materials were authentic and accurate in furnishing descriptive information. They were stable, unobtrusive, and objective since the researcher could not alter the data that was collected (Merriam, 2009, p. 155). By reviewing eleven textbooks, the researcher used data saturation and rich descriptions to address validity and reliability concerns. Further, the textbooks were available to anyone so others might readily replicate the study (Merriam, 2009). The researcher might not be able to make generalizations based on findings because a case study is particularistic and contextual. Rather, the researcher could describe the findings in detail in order to develop a theory about the phenomenon of Iran's positioning in the history of Western Civilization (University of Surrey, 2016).

CHAPTER 4

RESULTS

The purpose of this qualitative case study was to explore how a selected sample of college-level history textbooks place Iran and Iranians in the origins of Western Civilization. The study contributed to knowledge base and practical application. That is, educators and students would note a Judeo-Christian-Greco-Roman narrative is a limited study of the origins of Western Civilization (Parcel & Taylor, 2015; Arnn, 2014, p. 1; Le Gates, 2001, p. 19; p. 6; Papper, 1995, p. 131). Therefore, educators and authors of history books would properly position Iran in the origins of Western Civilization, which in turn would address the pro-world history advocates' challenging the relevancy of teaching Western Civilization (Ricketts et al., 2011). This chapter presents the analysis method and key findings obtained from reviewing eleven textbooks most commonly selected by American college faculty to teach history of Western Civilization (College Board, 2016).

Analysis Method

The researcher selected the following textbooks based on College Board's College-Level Examination Program's (CLEP) recent survey identifying the most popular Western Civilization history textbooks among American college faculty (College Board, 2016). CLEP listed thirteen textbooks on studying Western Civilization history. The researcher obtained the following nine from that CLEP list based on availability through either her employer's textbook vendors (electronic versions) or history department textbook supplies (in print versions):

- Cole, J., & Symes, C. (2017). *Western Civilizations: Their history and their culture.* New York, NY: W. W. Norton & Company, Inc. (electronic version) (updated edition to CLEP's Coffin and Stacey, *Western Civilizations, Brief Edition* (W. W. Norton));
- Hunt, L., Martin, T. R., Rosenwein, B. H., & Smith, B. G. (2017). *The making of the West: Peoples and cultures.* Boston, MA: Bedford/St. Martin's (electronic version);
- Kidner, F. L., Bucur, M., Mathisen, R., McKee, S., & Weeks, T. R. (2014). *Making Europe: the story of the West.* Boston, MA: Wadsworth (electronic version);
- King, M. L. (2000). *Western civilization: A social and cultural history.* Upper Saddle River, NJ: Prentice Hall (in print version);
- Kishlansky, M., Geary, P., & O'Brien, P. (2010). *Civilization in the West.* Upper Saddle River, NJ: Pearson (in print version);
- McKay, J. P., Hill, B. D., Buckler, J., Crowston, C. H., Wiesner-Hanks, M. E., & Perry, J. (2014). *A history of Western society.* Boston, MA: Bedford/St. Martin's (electronic version);
- Noble, T. F. X., Strauss, B., Osheim, D. J., Neuschel, K. B., Accampo, E. A., Roberts, D. D., & Cohen, W. B. (2011). *Western civilization: Beyond boundaries.* Boston, MA: Wadsworth (electronic version);
- Sherman, D., & Salisbury, J. (2014). *The West in the world: A history of Western civilization.* New York, NY: The McGraw-Hill Companies, Inc. (electronic version); and
- Spielvogel, J. J. (2015). *Western civilization.* Stamford, CT: Cengage Learning (electronic version).

The researcher also included the following textbooks that were not part of the CLEP list given they were also readily available through her employer's textbook vendors:

- Campbell, K. L. (2015). *Western Civilization: A global and comparative approach, Volume I: To 1715*. New York, NY: Routledge (electronic version), and
- Perry, M., Chase, M., Jacob, J. R., Jacob, M. C., Daly, J. W., & Von Laue, T. H. (2016). *Western civilization: Ideas, politics, and society*. Boston, MA: Cengage Learning (electronic version).

The researcher reviewed and collected expert opinion on the following five themes of interest involving the positioning of Iran and Iranians in the origins of Western Civilization: (1) terminology and definition of Iran, Iranians, and Iranian languages; (2) roots and origins of Iranian peoples; (3) which Iranian peoples are noted in general; (4) which Iranian peoples in ancient Europe are specifically noted; and (5) Iranians in connection with six unique Western Civilization attributes (based on classical legacy such as Greek philosophy, law and order, human rights, democracy, individualism, and Christianity). The researcher chose these themes based on her expertise in the field. In order to discover how history textbooks position Iran and Iranians in the origins of Western Civilization, one should search the content for terminology and definition, roots and ancestry, and cultural characteristics. The researcher chose the six unique Western traits in Theme 5 based on Huntington (1996) and Duchesne (2011). In this study, the collective expert opinion on each theme provided the control measures by which the researcher reviewed the content of the selected history textbooks.

In order to choose experts in accordance with the thematic approach, the researcher assumed the role of a textbook author. That is, if she were to write a textbook on Western Civilization history without omitting or marginalizing Iran's positioning then she would consult a diverse group of experts specializing in Iranian, Western Civilization, and Indo-European studies in order to formulate a consensus on each topic. The researcher provided a full list of experts in Appendix B. The researcher relied on her professional background as a historian specializing in Iranian studies to select search words under each theme that may lead to discovering what experts say about Iran. For example, based on her professional training, the researcher knows that Iran is a word derived from Aryan and that Iranians are an Indo-European people. Therefore, for Themes 1 and 2 focusing on the definition of Iran and origins of Iranians, respectively, the researcher listed the terms Aryan, Indo-European, and Indo-Iranians as words to search in expert opinion. These terms supplemented the more obvious search words—Iran and Iranians—and directed her to the content in the expert publication where she found rich definition of Iran and description of origins of Iranians. For Themes 3 and 4, the researcher used Vasseghi (2014) and Waldman and Mason (2006) to make a list of known Iranian peoples. The goal was to look up as many Iranian tribes as possible to minimize bias. For Greek philosophy as a Western trait under Theme 5, the researcher added peoples and places that related to early Greek philosophy such as Miletus, Pythagoras, Heraclitus, Anaxagoras, Socrates, Plato, and Aristotle. For law and order as a Western trait under Theme 5, the researcher added the terms Medism, Darius, and data. For human rights as a Western trait under Theme 5, the researcher added the terms Cyrus, Cyrus Cylinder, Code of Chivalry, and equality. For democracy as a Western trait under Theme 5, the researcher added the term Darius. For individualism as a Western trait under Theme 5, the researcher added the terms free will, choice, Zoroaster, and Zoroastrianism. For Christianity as a Western trait under Theme 5, the researcher added the terms Zoroaster, Zoroastrianism, Mithraism, Manichaeism, and Magi.

Once the researcher collected a rich category of definitions and descriptions for Themes 1, 2, and 5, she used different color highlighters to code the information in search of common elements among expert opinion. For example, for Themes 1 and 2, the researcher used pink highlighter for how experts defined Iran; green for how they defined Iranians; orange for how they defined Iranian languages; and blue for origins of Iranians. For Themes 3 and 4, the researcher excluded any Iranian tribes from the study for which less than three experts discussed them (such as, Allobroges, Antes, Ashvakas, Balkars, Corduchi, etc.). These experts designated the tribes as Iranian, Indo-Iranian, Iranian-speaker, or of Iranian country. The goal was to isolate the most popular and well-known Iranian tribes among experts given the surveyed textbooks targeted undergraduate education in introductory history courses. The researcher then placed the selected Iranian tribes under Themes 3 and 4 into a table in alphabetical order for straightforward search by tribal name and recordation of findings. For Theme 5, the researcher coded expert opinion on the six unique Western traits based on Iranian origins (pink color), Iranian influence (yellow color), and Iranian preservation (orange color) of said traits. For example, if an expert cited the Cyrus Cylinder as the first human rights decree, then the researcher highlighted that information in pink. If an expert discussed Thomas Jefferson's recommendations on studying the biography of Cyrus the Great, then the researcher highlighted that information in yellow. If an expert referred to Iranian preservation of ancient Greek intellectual works to safeguard them from a Christian Roman Empire's destruction, then the researcher highlighted that information in orange. The researcher provided the words used to search expert opinion on each theme under Presentation of Results section.

After the completion of expert opinion on the five themes, the researcher created tables for each theme based on expert opinion in order to collect data from the selected college history textbooks. The researcher looked for consensus among experts to formulate control measures from which commonly shared elements on the topics emerged. These searching parameters served as labels for columns in the tables while the row headers for all tables (except Themes 3 and 4) were by textbook author last name in alphabetical order. The researcher provided the expert opinions and extraction of searching parameters for each theme under Presentation of Results.

Presentation of Results

The researcher divided this section by Themes 1-5. Under each Theme, the researcher began with expert opinion on the topic followed by findings in selected college textbooks.

Theme 1—Terminology and Definition of Iran, Iranians, and Iranian languages

In this section, the researcher will present findings for the definition of each term—Iran, Iranians, and Iranian languages—separately.

Definition of Iran. The researcher looked up the words Iran, Iranians, Aryan, Indo-European, and Indo-Iranian in the Index or Glossary as well as appropriate sections of expert publications.

The word *Iran*, meaning Kingdom of the Aryans, derives from the root word *Ariya* or *Arya* (*Aryan*). Aryan is a self-designation by Indo-Iranian branch of the Indo-European linguistic family since antiquity. Ancient authors knew the term. The use of Aryan has a long history translated as ancestral nobility, a member of our group, nobleman, or us. In Indo-European studies, the term Aryan is exclusively used to mean the Iranian and the Indic (Vedic) branches (collectively, Indo-Iranian). Ethnically, geographically, and historically, Greater Iran refers to various peoples living across Iranian lands and speaking Iranian languages. Since ancient times Iranians dwelled in many places including parts of Transcaucasia, Central Asia, north-west India, Mesopotamia, the Iranian plateau (Afghanistan and Iran), and Europe. Westerners often use Persia as a proxy for Iran even though it specifically refers to the homeland of one of many Iranian tribes, the Persians, located in the southwestern part of the Iranian plateau. (Briant, 2002; Cook, 2003; Diakonoff, 2003a; Diakonoff, 2003b; Foltz, 2016; Fortson IV, 2004; Frye, 2004; Kuz'mina, 2007; Rashidvash, 2012; Samiei, 2014; Schmitt, 2011; Wisesehöfer, 2006; and Yamauchi, 1990/1996)

The researcher used the most commonly shared elements of this broad definition from among experts to analyze the definition of Iran in the selected college history textbooks.

Finding 1. Iran is a word derived from Aryan, and Aryan was a self-designation known in the Age of Antiquity. Campbell (2015) and Kishlansky, Geary, and O'Brien (2010) do not mention the word Aryan. The other nine surveyed textbooks put the word and the concept Aryan or Aryan race under a 19th c. mythical or fictional racist notion used by 20th c. Nazism to promote Germanic, white European, or non-Jewish (Semitic) superiority. Six of eleven surveyed textbooks asserted an Aryan race or Aryan people did not exist, Aryan race is mythical, or Aryans lost their identity by mixing with others (Cole & Symes, 2017; Hunt, Martin, Rosenwein, & Smith, 2017; King, 2000; Perry et al., 2016; Sherman & Salisbury, 2014; and Spielvogel, 2015). Only King (2000) noted that Iran is a word derived from Aryan and that some Indo-Europeans such as the Indic, who settled in India, called themselves Aryan (p. 55). Although King (2000) claimed that the Medes and the Persians of Iran were Indo-European, it is not clear from the content whether Iranians called themselves Aryans. Kidner, Bucur, Mathisen, McKee, and Weeks (2014) explained that Aryans were Indo-Europeans who settled in Iran and India (pp. 14, 53).

Finding 2. Aryan means ancestral nobility, a member of our group, nobleman, or us.
King (2000) and Noble et al. (2011) defined the word Aryan as honor or liberty and noble, respectively, but attributed it to an Indic/Sanskrit definition.

Finding 3. Aryan refers exclusively to the Iranian and Indic branches of Indo-Europeans. King (2000) noted that today Aryan designates the Indo-Iranian branch of Indo-European languages or, more narrowly, those who invaded India (Indic). King (2000), Noble et al. (2011), and Perry et al. (2016) claimed Aryan formerly meant the Indo-European language family or considered as a possible source for modern Indo-European languages.

Finding 4. Greater Iran refers to lands inhabited by Iranian speaking peoples across Asia and Europe. With respect to the concept of a Greater Iran, the surveyed textbooks that made reference to the size and scope of an Iranian empire only covered the Achaemenid Persian Empire (550-330 BCE). That is, King (2000), Noble et al. (2011), Perry et al. (2016), and Spielvogel (2015) categorized the Achaemenid Persian Empire as the ancient world's greatest or largest empire.

Finding 5. The word Persia is often a proxy for Iran. Seven of the eleven surveyed textbooks referred to Persia as modern Iran (Campbell, 2015; Hunt et al., 2017; King, 2000; McKay et al., 2014; Noble et al., 2011; Perry et al., 2016; Sherman & Salisbury, 2014), but only Perry et al. (2016) explained that modern Iranians are descendants of ancient Persians (p. 24).

Definition of Iranians. The researcher looked up the words Iran, Iranians, Aryan, Indo-European, and Indo-Iranian in the Index or Glossary as well as appropriate sections of expert publications.

Iranian peoples are Indo-European and linguistically divided into Eastern and Western branches. Iranians dwelled in Asia and Europe since antiquity. There are many Iranian tribes, but sources often use the name of the famous Persian tribe as a proxy for Iranian. Iranian refers to the linguistic classification as well as peoples living across Iranian lands. In order to learn about Iranian culture, it is imperative to include the following modern territories: Afghanistan, Pakistan, Turkmenistan, Uzbekistan, Tajikistan, and Kirghizistan. (Brosius, 2006; Dabashi, 2015; Diakonoff, 2003b; Frye, 2012; Hanks, Epimakhov and Renfrew, 2007; Samiei, 2014; Wisesehöfer, 2006; and Yamauchi, 1990/1996)

The researcher used the most commonly shared elements of this broad definition from among experts to analyze the definition of Iranians in the selected college history textbooks.

Finding 1. Iranians are Indo-Europeans. Campbell (2015) does not mention Indo-Europeans. Hunt, Martin, Rosenwein, and Smith (2017) stated Medes are an Iranian people (p. 37) and Iranians are non-Arabs (p. 898). According to Kidner et al. (2014), the Medes and the Persians are Aryans of the Indo-European family (p. 53). Cole and Symes (2017) described the Medes of Iran as Indo-European. Seven of eleven surveyed textbooks labeled both Medes and Persians of Iran as Indo-European peoples (King, 2000; Kishlansky, Geary, & O'Brien, 2010; McKay et al., 2014; Noble et al., 2011; Perry et al., 2016; Sherman & Salisbury, 2014, and Spielvogel, 2015).

Finding 2. In addition to Asia, Iranians inhabited Europe in the Age of Antiquity. Campbell (2015) and Spielvogel (2015) noted the Persians conquered Thrace and Macedonia. Hunt et al. (2017) stated the Persians conquered the eastern edge of Europe. Kidner et al. (2014) claimed, "Persian occupation of Thrace marked the first time a Near Eastern empire had occupied territory in Europe" (p. 57).

Finding 3. There are many Iranian tribes. McKay et al. (2014) referred to the Medes being an Iranian people closely related to the Persians, and Hunt et al. (2017) called the Medes an Iranian people. Perry et al. (2016) claimed the Iranians today are descendants of ancient Persians (p. 24).

Definition of Iranians languages. The researcher looked up the words Iran, Iranians, Indo-European, and Indo-Iranian in the Index or Glossary as well as appropriate sections of expert publications.

Iranian languages fall under the Indo-European family and are European in origin. Proto-Indo-Iranian languages emerged in Central Asia by third or early second millennium BCE. The Indo-Iranian branch split between 1700-1500 BCE. Examples of Iranian languages are Avestan, Median, Persian, Saka/Scythian, Parthian, Sogdian, Alan, Pashto, Kurdish, Baluchi, and Khotanese. Under the Indo-European umbrella, the Iranian languages are second oldest group after Anatolian. Today some 150-200 million people speak one of 87 Iranian languages. Sources may use Persian dialect interchangeably with Iranian languages in general, but Persian was not the commonly spoken Iranian language. In the Age of Antiquity, Iranian speakers lived across Western China to Western Europe. (Boyce, 1987; Briant, 2002; Brosius, 2006; Dabashi, 2015; Daryaee, 2008; Diakonoff, 2003a; Diakonoff, 2003b; Foltz, 2016; Fortson IV, 2004; Frye, 2004; Gamkrelidze & Ivanov, 1990; Kuz'mina, 2007; Mallory, 1989; Rashidvash, 2012; Renfrew, 1990; Schmitt, 2011; Skjærvø, 2012; Stopler, 2005; Windfuhr, 2000; and Yamauchi, 1990/1996)

The researcher used the most commonly shared elements of this broad definition from among experts to analyze the definition of Iranian languages in the selected college history textbooks.

Finding 1. Iranian is an Indo-European language. Campbell (2015) does not mention Indo-Europeans. Cole and Symes (2017), King (2000), Kishlansky et al. (2010), and Perry et al. (2016) stated the Persian language is Indo-European. McKay et al. (2014) and Noble et al. (2011) claimed both Persians and Medes are Indo-European speakers. Sherman and Salisbury (2014) listed Iranian language as Indo-European (p. G-6) while Spielvogel's (2015) chart on Indo-European languages showed Indo-Iranian with a subgroup Persian language (p. 29). Hunt et al. (2017) and Kidner et al. (2014) discussed Indo-European family but left out Iranian languages.

Finding 2. There are currently many Iranian languages with millions of speakers. Campbell (2015) explained that Hindi and Urdu are a Persian blend and Kidner et al. (2014) categorized Tadjik language as related to Persian.

Theme 2—Roots and Origins of Iranian Peoples

The researcher looked up the words Iran, Iranians, Indo-European, and Indo-Iranian in the Index or Glossary as well as appropriate sections of expert publications.

The proto-Indo-Europeans were a Neolithic, pastoralist society that originated in the eastern central part of Europe by fourth to early third millennium BCE. The Indo-Europeans moved from the center to the peripheral areas spreading to the Atlantic in the west, the Bay of Bengal in the east, the Polar Sea in the north, and the Mediterranean in the south. The proto-Indo-Iranian branch split around third millennium BCE and moved in waves across Central Asia and then the Iranian Plateau by second millennium BCE. They took two routes during their migration: (1) the Caucasian route and (2) through Central Asia. In Iranian traditions, the ancient homeland of Iranians is *Airyanam Vaejo* meaning Land of the Aryans that was probably by the Ural Mountains near Siberia. The

Ural Mountains play a key role in linking Eastern Europe, Central Asia, and Western Siberia. By 1200, BCE there was an undeniable Iranian presence in the Iranian Plateau. They gradually overwhelmed the local population, notably the ancient civilizations of the Elamites in southwest Iran, the Lullubians in western Iran, and the Jiroft or Helmand Cultures in eastern Iran (possibly an extension of the pre-Indo-European Indus Valley civilization in the neighboring Indian subcontinent). Iranians also settled in South-East Europe and Central Asia. Experts may classify Iran as Caucasoid with all three groups of Nordics, Alpines, and Mediterranean present. The Alpines or round-heads dominate. The following Bronze Age archaeological cultural sites are Indo-Iranian or Iranian: Pit-grave cultures such as Tripolye group (Ukraine) and Sintashta type (Russia), Timber-grave (Ukraine), Andronovo (Siberia), Bishkent (Tajikistan), and Tazabagyab (Aral Sea in Central Asia). Ancient Iranians engaged in agriculture, stock raising, and making gold, copper, and bronze artifacts. Numerous ancient weapons have Iranian names. Additionally, ancient Iranians were influential in the spread of horse-breeding and horse-drawn chariots. (Briant, 2002; Cortesi, Tosi, Lazzari, &Vidale, 2008; Daryaee, 2008; Diakonoff, 2003a; Diakonoff, 2003b; Farrokh, 2007; Foltz, 2016; Frye, 2004; Hanks, Epimakhov & Renfrew, 2007; Kozintsev, 2008; Kristinsson, 2012; Kuz'mina, 2007; Rashidvash, 2012; Samiei, 2014; Skjærvø, 2012; Windfuhr, 2000; and Yamauchi, 1990/1996)

The researcher used the most commonly shared elements of this broad description from among experts to analyze roots and origins of Iranians in the surveyed college history textbooks.

Proto-Indo-Iranians, Airyanam Vaejo, and the Iranian Plateau. The researcher searched the textbooks in the study for the origins and migrations of proto-Indo-Iranians, discussions about the ancient Iranian homeland, and the migration patterns of Iranians to the Iranian Plateau.

Finding 1. The proto-Indo-Iranian branch split around third millennium BCE and moved in waves to Central Asia and the Iranian Plateau. Spielvogel (2015) suggested original Indo-Europeans occupied the steppe region north of the Black Sea, modern Iran, or Afghanistan (p. 28). Campbell (2015) and Kishlansky et al. (2010) did not mention origins or migrations of Iranians or Indo-Europeans. Cole and Symes (2017) and Hunt et al. (2017) discussed Indo-Europeans and/or their migrations in general, but not with respect to Iran or Iranians.

Finding 2. Iranians called their ancient homeland Airyanam Vaejo meaning land of the Aryans that may have been by the Ural Mountains near Siberia. None of the surveyed textbooks discussed this topic.

Finding 3. Iranians dominated the Iranian Plateau by 1200 BCE. According to Kidner et al. (2014), "the earliest known Indo-European migration occurred around 2000 B.C.E. One group, the Aryans, settled in modern day Iran" (p. 14). King (2000), Perry et al. (2016), Sherman and Salisbury (2014), and Spielvogel (2015) noted that by 2000 B.C.E. groups of Indo-Europeans migrated to places such as Iran or Persia. McKay et al. (2014) claimed "Iran's geographical position and topography explain its traditional role as the highway between western and eastern Asia," and that "Iran became the area where nomads met urban dwellers. Among the nomadic groups was Indo-European speaking peoples who migrated into this area about 1000 B.C.E." (p. 52). Noble et al. (2011) stated that the Indo-European Medes and Persians arrived in Iran between 1500-900 B.C.E.

Themes 3 and 4—Coverage of Iranian Peoples

Since Theme 4 was a subsection of Theme 3, the researcher combined the results for the two themes here. The researcher created a table listing a sample of known Iranian peoples based on Vasseghi (2014) and Waldman and Mason (2006). The goal was to look up as many Iranian tribes as possible to minimize bias. The researcher consulted expert publications to show the extent to which they designated these tribes as Iranian, Indo-Iranian, Iranian-speaker, or of Iranian country (see Appendix C). The researcher then searched the surveyed college textbooks to see what they said about the 27 selected Iranian tribes (nineteen inhabitants of Asia and eight inhabitants of Europe in the Age of Antiquity).

Selected Iranian inhabitants of Asia. The following findings involved the nineteen selected Iranian inhabitants of Asia—Arachosian, Arian, Bactrian, Baluch, Caspian, Chorasmian, Kurd, Massagetae, Mede, Mitanni, Pallava/Pahlavi, Pamir, Parsis, Parthian, Pashtun, Persian, Saggarthian, Sogdian, and Tajik. The researcher analyzed the coverage of the nineteen selected Asiatic Iranians in the surveyed college history textbooks.

Finding 1. None of the surveyed textbooks mentioned the tribes Arian, Baluch, Caspian, Pallava/Pahlavi, Pashtun, and Saggarthian. Some of the surveyed textbooks mentioned or noted on a map without identification the tribes Arachosian, Chorasmian, Massagetae, Pamir, and Sogdian. Therefore, none of the eleven surveyed textbooks mentioned or identified 11 out of 19 of the selected Asiatic Iranian tribes.

Finding 2. With respect to the remaining eight Asiatic Iranian tribes as selected, none of the surveyed textbooks identified Bactrians as Iranian peoples. Kidner et al. (2014) and McKay et al. (2014) referred to Bactria as modern day Afghanistan while McKay et al. (2014) explained that they were once part of the Persian Empire.

None of the surveyed textbooks identified the Kurds as Iranian people. McKay et al. (2014) called them non-Arabs and Spielvogel (2014) referred to them as an ethnic people.

None of the textbooks in the study identified the Mitanni as Iranian. Campbell (2015) and Spielvogel (2015) called them a regional power while Cole and Symes (2017) referred to them as a people. King (2000) suggested the Mitannis probably originated from Armenia.

Kidner et al. (2014) and McKay et al. (2014) mentioned the Parsis, but as Zoroastrians who migrated to India. The textbooks in the study did not identify the Parsis as of Iranian descent.

Kidner et al. (2014) claimed the Tajiks and the Persians are related, and Sherman and Salisbury (2014) called the Tajiks an ethnic group.

Noble et al. (2011) referred to the Parthians as a Persian dynasty. Cole and Symes (2017), Hunt et al. (2017), and McKay et al. (2014) claimed they ruled Persia. Kidner et al. (2014) stated they were an Indo-European people who occupied Iran while King (2000) said they were an Asian people from Caspian region who settled in Iran. None of the textbooks in the study identified the Parthians as an Iranian people.

Seven surveyed textbooks called the Medes an Indo-European people of Iran (Cole & Symes, 2017; King, 2000; Kishlansky et al., 2010; Noble et al., 2011; Perry et al., 2016; Sherman & Salisbury, 2014; and Spielvogel, 2015). Hunt et al. (2017) and McKay et al. (2014) identified the Medes as an Iranian people. Kidner et al. (2014) specified that they were Indo-European Aryans in Iran.

Campbell (2015), Cole and Symes (2017), Hunt et al. (2017), Kishlansky et al. (2010) did not identify the Persians as Iranians. Kidner et al. (2014) claimed the Persians were Indo-European Aryans in Iran. Five textbooks in the study said they were Indo-Europeans (King,

2000; Noble et al., 2011; Perry et al., 2016; Sherman & Salisbury, 2014; and Spielvogel, 2015). McKay et al. (2014) noted that the Persians were an Iranian people closely related to the Medes.

Selected Iranian inhabitants of Europe. The following findings involved the eight selected Iranian inhabitants of Europe—Alan, Aorsi, Cimmerian, Iazyges/Jasz, Ossetian, Roxolani, Saka/Scythian, and Sarmatian/Sauromatian. The researcher analyzed the coverage of the eight selected European Iranians in the surveyed college history textbooks.

Finding 1. None of the textbooks in the study mentioned 4 out of 8 selected European Iranian tribes Aorsi, Cimmerian, Iazyges/Jasz, and Roxolani.

Finding 2. With respect to the remaining four European Iranian tribes as selected, McKay et al. (2014) identified the Alans as Central Asian nomads who played a factor in Germanic peoples' migrations while Perry et al. (2016) discussed their alliance with the Goths against the Romans. McKay et al. (2014) and Noble et al. (2011) mentioned Ossetians in current political affairs without identification. King (2000) described Sarmatian/Sauromatians as "other peoples" near the Black Sea who tried to take over Persia (p. 223). None of the textbooks identified the Alans, Ossetians, and Sarmatian/Sauromatians as Iranians.

Kidner et al. (2014) called the Saka/Scythian tribe Indo-European nomads of Central Asia (p. 51), King (2000) labeled them as a nomadic people in Asia Minor, southern Russia, and Black Sea region (p. 70), and Noble et al. (2011) referred to them as a "tough nomadic people in Ukraine" (p. 36). As far as the historical role of the Saka/Scythian tribe, Kidner et al. (2014) stated they were part of the alliance that defeated the Assyrians, they fought the Persians, and Paul's Christian sermons mentioned them. King (2000) and McKay et al. (2014) showed Scythian jewelry while Noble et al. (2011) cited ancient sources about the women in Attila the Hun's campaigns singing Scythian songs (p. 181). Both King (2000) and Perry et al. (2016)

explained that the Scythian slave force served as an Athenian police force. None of the surveyed textbooks identified the Saka/Scythian as Iranian.

Theme 5—Iranians in Connection with Six Unique Western Civilization Attributes

The researcher divided Theme 5 further down by selected six unique Western traits. Under each unique Western trait, the researcher presented expert opinion on the topic followed by findings in selected textbooks.

Greek philosophy as a unique Western trait. The researcher looked up the words Greek philosophy, philosophy, Miletus, Pythagoras, Heraclitus, Anaxagoras, Socrates, Plato, and Aristotle for the following description based on expert opinion.

Greek philosophy flourished under the Achaemenid Persian Empire (550-330 BCE) (Wisesehöfer, 2006). Greeks partially constructed their philosophy out of their interactions with non-Greeks (Vasunia, 2007). As early as fifth century BCE, Greeks were familiar and fascinated with Iranian prophet and philosopher Zoroaster, dating him before 6000 BCE (Clark, 2001; Vasunia, 2007). Although dating Zoroaster is difficult, Boyce (1987) suggested 1400-1200 BCE and Clark (2001) stated roughly 1400 BCE as viewed by "a large number of scholars" (p. 1). Greek intellectuals appealed to Zoroaster for different reasons. They portrayed him as a magi, prophet, philosopher, and astrologer. In antiquity, people knew the Iranian Zoroastrian priestly class as the Magi (Foltz, 2016; Russell, 1992; Razmjou, 2005; Clark, 2001; Diakonoff, 2003b, p. 141).

Disciples of Pythagoras and Plato invoked Zoroaster in their works. There was strong receptivity to Iranian influences in Greece, the Aegean, and Anatolia (Vasunia, 2007). "Iranian influence on classical Greek and Roman culture is not just plausible but likely" (Vasunia, 2007, p. 242). Aristoxenus discussed the fundamental dualism in

Zoroastrian thought. Aristoxenus, Endemus of Rhodes, Apuleius, and Clement of Alexandria claimed that Pythagoras was a student of Zoroaster's especially regarding dualism. Even Augustine and Pliny referred to the encounter between Pythagoras and Zoroaster (Vasunia, 2007). The dualism concept of good versus evil is central to Iranian Zoroastrian, not Greek or Jewish philosophies. By the Hellenistic period, both the Greek and Hebrew texts show strong familiarity with Iranian dualism (Russell, 1992). Aristotle also described the Zoroastrian dualistic doctrine (Yamauchi, 1990/1996; Russell, 1992). Greek historian Theopompus as well as Plutarch and Diogenes Laertius also discussed Iranian dualism (Vasunia, 2007).

Plato allegedly made Iranian wisdom very fashionable. Zoroaster was an important element in Greek attempt to stake out a privileged space for learning and philosophy. Colotes of Lampsacus argued that with respect to the myth of Er, Plato plagiarized Zoroaster (Vasunia, 2007). In Hellenistic learning, Zoroaster provided authority and relevant wisdom. The contact between Greeks and Iranians after the Greco-Persian wars was "solid and irrefutable" making it a lived experience for many Greeks (Vasunia, 2007, p. 253). Philosopher Heraclides of Pontus and Xenophon expressed different opinions about Iranian model of pleasure (Lenfant, 2007). By the end of antiquity, ancient intellectuals attributed many books and treatises to Zoroaster. One may note the influence of Zoroastrianism among the major pre-Socratic philosophers such as Pherecydes of Syros, Heraclitus, Anaximander, and Empedocles (Vasunia, 2007, p. 253). The Greeks considered the Iranian Zoroastrian priests, the Magi, to have knowledge of stones and plants for medicinal purposes (Briant, 2002). Pliny and Diogenes reported that Persian king Xerxes left the Magi in Greek city of Abdera as tutors for philosopher

Democritus (Briant, 2002). Themistocles also became familiar with the Magi teachings at the Persian Court. Xenophon's Oeconomicus uses Iranian ideas about a good king having agricultural know-how to convey the "importance of war and agriculture" (Briant, 2002, p. 233). Xenophon's Cyropaedia (Education of Cyrus) was an historical and philosophical work on the career of an ideal leader, the 6th c. BCE Persian king Cyrus the Great, and how the Persian government by the elite is desirable for Athens (Danzig, 2007; Briant, 2002). Plato's Laws presented Cyrus as having reached the perfect balance in governance (Briant, 2002).

In 529, under Persian king Khosrow I Anushiravan's hospitality, the Neoplatonic philosophers found refuge in the Persian Empire after having had their Academy shut down by the Roman Emperor Justinian I (Foltz, 2016; Wisesehöfer, 2006). When the Neoplatonic philosophers became homesick, King Khosrow negotiated their safe return to Athens with Emperor Justinian. The Persian king supported a medical school that taught Greek theories and translated and preserved Greek and Sanskrit works in the Persian language. (Frye, 2003, p. 161)

The researcher used the most commonly shared elements of this broad description from among experts to analyze Iranians in connection with Greek philosophy as a unique Western trait in the surveyed college history textbooks.

Finding 1. The flourishing of Greek philosophy under the Achaemenid Persian Empire. All eleven textbooks in the study pointed to Miletus (an Ionia city) and/or Ionia (in Asia Minor) as the birthplace of Greek philosophy by sixth century BCE. Campbell (2015), Kidner et al. (2014), Kishlansky et al. (2010), and Spielvogel (2015) stated by sixth century BCE Ionia was under Persian rule. Most of the textbooks in the study claimed that Egyptian, Babylonian, and

Near Eastern influences shaped early Greek philosophy in Ionian region. Nine out of eleven surveyed textbooks listed rationalism or reason as the unique Greek contribution to philosophy and science. Sherman & Salisbury (2014) stated Greeks changed Mesopotamian views in looking at humans as active players in the world. Perry et al. (2016) claimed the Sophists answered a need in Athens after its transformation due to the Greco-Persian Wars, and that the Classical Age of Greece—during which the arts, architecture, science, and philosophy truly flourished—was a response to the Greek victory in the Greco-Persians Wars. Cole and Symes (2017) noted that Near Eastern traditions influenced early Ionian Greek philosophers as seen in how some "echoed the vaunting rhetoric of Persian imperial decrees" (p. 72). Kidner et al. (2014) noted that the Greco-Persian confrontation beginning sixth century BCE was "one of the most important focal points" in Western Civilization history (p. 57).

Finding 2. Zoroaster and his teachings such as cosmic dualism (good versus evil). Kishlansky et al. (2010) was the only textbook that did not cover Zoroastrianism. Cole and Symes (2017) and Kidner et al. (2014) claimed Greeks knew of Zoroaster. Six out of eleven surveyed textbooks dated Zoroaster or the spread of Zoroastrianism to sixth century BCE (Campbell, 2015; Cole & Symes, 2017; King, 2000; McKay et al., 2014; Sherman & Salisbury, 2014; and Spielvogel, 2015). Kidner et al. (2014) dated Zoroaster to eighth century BCE and Perry et al. (2016) stated that Zoroaster's date might be earlier than sixth century BCE. McKay et al. (2014) explained that Zoroaster's dates are unknown but his teachings were prominent by sixth century BCE while Noble et al. (2014) claimed Zoroaster has an obscure beginning but may have emerged between 10th and 6th c. BCE. With the exception of Kishlansky et al. (2010), the other ten textbooks covered Zoroaster's philosophical views known as dualism—cosmic battle between good and evil—as a new way of explaining the world. Almost all of the textbooks emphasized Zoroaster's teachings on people having free will, personal responsibility, and the freedom to choose between good versus bad, including morality, ethical thinking, reflecting with a clear mind rather than superstition, abstract ideas about two states of being (spiritual and material), and the problem of evil in the context of religion. McKay et al. (2014), Sherman and Salisbury (2014), and Spielvogel (2015) called Zoroaster's teachings new, original, and unique.

Finding 3. The role of the Magi. Campbell (2015), Hunt et al. (2017), Kishlansky et al. (2010), and Perry et al. (2016) did not cover the Magi. The other seven surveyed textbooks defined Magi as Zoroastrian or Iranian (Median/Persian) priests or teachers. Noble et al. (2011) noted that to the West, the Magi were wise and virtuous. Sherman and Salisbury (2014) claimed the Magi were celebrated Persian astrologers.

Finding 4. Greek writers and philosophers on Iranian thought and ideals. Only three textbooks mention Herodotus as an Ionian Greek born in the Persian Empire or having direct experience with the Persians (Campbell, 2015; Cole & Symes, 2017; McKay et al., 2014). Cole and Symes (2017) and Sherman and Salisbury (2014) mentioned Pythagoras having fled Ionia for southern Italy after the Persian conquest. King (2000) stated that Pythagoras used Egyptian and Babylonian works, Noble et al. (2011) explained Pythagoras himself had claimed knowledge of Mesopotamian traditions, and Sherman and Salisbury (2014) added Pythagoras spread Asian and Greek sciences in southern Italy. Kidner et al. (2014) and Sherman and Salisbury (2014) noted that Greek historian Xenophon wrote about his experiences as a mercenary in the Persian army. With respect to following different ideas, Sherman and Salisbury (2014) claimed those living in the Roman Empire followed Persian philosophical and religious views and others such as first century author Apuleius who was a magician and a Platonist. Finally, King (2000) stated that thinkers from the Hellenistic period (323-31 BCE) became familiar with Babylonian and Egyptian sciences.

Finding 5. Neoplatonic School and Iran. Cole and Symes (2017), Kidner et al. (2014), and Perry et al. (2016) mentioned Justinian's orders to shut the academy but did not say anything about Iran's role in the situation. Hunt et al. (2017) and King (2000) discussed the closing of the schools under Justinian and Persia's acceptance of the exiled philosophers.

Finding 6. Translations and preservation of ancient Greek works. Campbell (2015) said nothing about translation and preservation of Greek knowledge after the rise and spread of Christianity. The other ten surveyed textbooks attributed the ultimate preservation and transmittal of ancient Greek philosophy and science to early medieval Muslims/Arabs/Islamic civilization. Kidner et al. (2014) noted that the key commentator on Aristotle's works that was transmitted to the West was a Persian scholar named Avicenna (11th c.) although Sherman and Salisbury (2014) categorized the influential Avicenna as a Muslim scholar. McKay et al. (2014), Noble et al. (2011), and Sherman and Salisbury (2014) stated Greek and Persian works were codified and translated to Arabic under medieval Muslim rulers before being passed on to the West. Perry et al. (2016) explained that Arabs did not have any tradition of science or philosophy but absorbed and translated the teachings of Greeks and Persians and accessed Greek knowledge through Persian and Byzantine civilizations that had preserved Greek heritage. King (2000) was the only textbook that claimed Persia was one of the places that sheltered Greek knowledge from Christian emperors.

Law and order as a unique Western trait. The researcher looked up the words law and order, Medism, Darius, and data for the following description based on expert opinion.

Herodotus admired the Persian King Cyrus the Great. In Cyropaedia, Xenophon presented Cyrus as an ideal ruler. Greeks also saw him as a lawgiver (Time-Life, 1995). In an October 6, 1820 letter, Thomas Jefferson advised his grandson to study Cyropaedia among other classical works (The Metropolitan Museum of Art, 2013). According to Herodotus, Cyrus had a negative view of Greek markets where people are deceived (Burn, 2003).

Plato considered the Persian king Darius the Great as a great lawgiver, because he recognized the importance of codified law (Cook, 2003; Time-Life, 1995). The Old Testament characterized the Iranian conquest of Babylon as a blessing (Brosius, 2006; Clark, 2001). The biblical book Daniel claimed that the Persian kings were not above the law of the Medes and the Persians (Frye, 2004; Time-Life, 1995). Persian rulers were merciless to corrupt politicians (Time-Life, 1995). Greek authors emphasized the importance of justice to the Iranians. The Armenians, Jews, and Akkadians adopted the Persian word *data* meaning "laws or regulations" (Briant, 2005; Frye, 2004; Oppenhein, 2003).

The Persian Empire "created the first unified empire reaching from the Indus to the Mediterranean" and was "a decisive phase in the development of the ancient Near East" (Briant, 1999, p. 105). The Iranian administration had to be "highly sophisticated and efficient" in order to manage the Achaemenid Persian Empire (Brosius, 2006, 0p. 47). One of Cyrus the Great's most ingenious innovations was to install a *satrap* (Old Persian meaning governor) to head each conquered land (Brosius, 2006; Briant, 2002). Frye (2004) noted that under the Achaemenid Persian Empire the people of Israel adopted the Torah as the law (p. 135). Many Greeks in Asia Minor preferred the Iranian suzerainty rather than the cutthroat Greek political interactions (Mallowan, 2003). In fifth century BCE, when the Persians put down the Ionian Revolt, they also restored law and order. Greeks criminalized Medism or "political collaboration with the Iranian government and its representatives" (Briant, 2002, p. 25).

Alexander the Great and the Seleucid Empire (312-63 BCE) adopted the Iranian political ideas and concepts (Wisesehöfer, 2006) such as the satrapal system, Persian gold daric, and a network of royal roads that glued the empire together (Hamitlon, 1999). The Persian administration tightened the Royal Road security by installing checkpoints to ensure safety (Time-Life, 1995). Alexander also adopted Iranian concepts such as making alliances with the local elites and respecting local sanctuaries and cults (Briant, 2005, p. 17). The Achaemenid Persian Empire served as an example for the later Greek and Roman empires (Time-Life, 1995).

In his poem *Vou-me embora pra Pasárgada* (I'm leaving for Pasargadae), Brazil's greatest Modernist poet Manuel Bandeira (1886-1968) equated the ancient Persian capital Pasargadae with Camelot—a term that is defined by Merriam-Webster Dictionary (2016) as "1: the site of King Arthur's palace and court; 2: the time, place, or atmosphere of idyllic happiness." People are very familiar with the story of King Arthur and the knights of Camelot. According to Littleton and Malcor (2000), the Arthurian legends "had one of the greatest influences on modern [Western] culture" (p. xiii). These stories equate Arthur with law and order (England, 2005, p. 18). Arthur, Lancelot, and the Arthurian legends including the holy sword, kingdom, and the Holy Grail are Iranian in origin (Littleton & Malcor, 2000; Brzezinski & Mielczarek, 2002). According to Nickel (1973-1974), many of the Sarmatian and Alanic traditions, such as the worship of a tribal god in the form of a sword stuck in a stone, resemble the Arthurian legends (p. 151). In Britain, the title of the commander of the Roman Legio VI Victrix under whom the Sarmatian knights served was Lucius Artorius Castus. It may be that in time the name Artorius turned into a title similar to Caesar. Out of a list of battles reportedly fought by Arthur, three were Sarmatian garrisons (Nickel, 1973-1974, p. 151). The name of Arthur's legendary sword Excalibur comes from a Greek word derived from the name of a Sarmatian tribe—Kalybes (Nickel, 1973-1974, p. 151). The management and organization of late Antiquity through early Medieval era Europe in bringing law and order after the fall of the Western Roman Empire are closely tied to the Frankish Merovingian and Carolingian dynasties. In Gaul, under the Visigoths and the later Merovingian dynasty, descendants of Alans played a role in gathering law codes and maintaining law and order (Bachrach, 1973). The Merovingian dynasty favored Iranian (Alan tribe) advisors. Members of the Carolingian dynasty of early Medieval Europe were descendants of the Iranian Alans (Littleton & Malcor, 2000, p. 33).

The researcher used the most commonly shared elements of this broad description from among experts to analyze Iranians in connection with law and order as a unique Western trait in the surveyed college history textbooks.

Finding 1. Iranian kings Cyrus and Darius as lawgivers. Persian king Cyrus the Great reversed the policies of previous empires such as the Assyrians by allowing other peoples to practice their own cultural and religious ways (Cole & Symes, 2017; Kidner, Bucur, Mathisen, McKee, & Weeks, 2014; Sherman & Salisbury, 2014). Cyrus was seen as a benevolent restorer, savior, or the anointed one (Hunt et al., 2017; Kidner et al., 2014; McKay et al., 2014; Sherman & Salisbury, 2014; Spielvogel, 2015). Cyrus knew how to govern peoples effectively through sound judgment, benevolence, tolerance, and keen interest in foreign peoples' ways of life (McKay et al., 2014, p. 55). According to Spielvogel (2015), Cyrus "must have been an unusual ruler for his time" given his wisdom and compassion (p. 43). Persian king Darius the Great was a gifted and efficient administrator whose policies ensured the long-term survival of the empire (Cole & Symes, 2017; Kidner et al., 2014; King, 2000; Spielvogel, 2015). Noble et al. (2011) quoted a royal inscription by Darius in which the Persian king claimed he did not follow Lies or wrongdoing because he was righteous (p. 38).

Finding 2. The historical significance of the Achaemenid Persian Empire. All textbooks described some aspects of the significance of the Achaemenid Persian Empire (550-330 BCE) and its early founders. To the ancient world, the Persian government was a superpower or the largest empire the world had seen and its kings known as the "Great King" or "King of Kings" (Cole & Symes, 2017; Hunt et al., 2017; King, 2000; Noble et al., 2011; Sherman & Salisbury, 2014; Spielvogel, 2015). Campbell (2015) and McKay et al. (2014) stated the Greeks admired the stability of the Persian politics, its kings, or its institutions; and Kishlansky et al. (2010) added that many Greeks viewed the Persians as allies or even preferred rulers (pp. 57-58). Noble et al. (2011) noted that the Persian Empire was the greatest success yet of a universal kingship.

Cole and Symes (2017), Kidner et al. (2014), and Spielvogel (2015) emphasized how the peoples viewed the Persian imperial policies as light-handed and lenient. Hunt et al. (2017), King (2000), McKay et al. (2014), Noble et al. (2011), Perry et al. (2016), and Spielvogel (2015) stated unlike previous empires, the Persian government won their subjects' loyalty with tolerance and respect for local laws and customs. King (2000) additionally declared that the Persian imperial policy of tolerance of ethnic and cultural diversity was a new value in the ancient world

(p. 53). Noble et al. (2011) called the Persian Empire "vast, prosperous, and law-abiding" (p. 34). King (2000) asserted, "Persians excelled at domination" because of their toleration policy (p. 53). "Jews actively sought political liberation from the Persians and their successors" (Kishlansky et al., 2010, p. 26), and expressed gratitude for being subjects of the Great Kings of Persia (Spielvogel, 2015, p. 51).

Hunt et al. (2017), Noble et al. (2011), and Perry et al. (2016) claimed the Persians placed their imperial polices on maintaining peace, rule of law, and order. Kidner et al. (2014) stated the Persian Empire had an "effective system of administration" (p. 58) based on "political unity and cultural diversity" (McKay et al., 2014, p. 52). Kidner et al. (2014), Noble et al. (2011), and Spielvogel (2015) explained that Persian policies were efficient because they were directed at facilitating trade and communication by ensuring safety on an unprecedented large-scale road system, increasing economic prosperity via standardized coin system, encouraging construction projects such as canals, building an imperial navy, standardizing law codes to minimize confusion, simplifying cuneiform system, and using a universal language (Aramaic). Both Noble et al. (2011) and Spielvogel (2015) claimed that the Achaemenid Persian Empire brought "relative peace" to the ancient world for more than two centuries (550 330 BCE).

Finding 3. The law of the Medes and the Persians and the Old Testament. None of the eleven surveyed textbooks covered the law of the Medes and the Persians.

Finding 4. Iranian satrapal system. The satrapal system was a Persian administrative design to carry out imperial policies of law and order. It was managed by Persian provincial governors loyal to the central government, who worked with local elites to keep peace and prosperity based on regional political and religious preferences (Campbell, 2015; Cole & Symes,

2017; Kidner et al., 2014; King, 2000; Noble et al., 2011; Perry et al., 2016; Sherman & Salisbury, 2014; Spielvogel, 2015).

Finding 5. Medism punishable under Greek laws. None of the eleven surveyed textbooks covered the Greek legal idea of Medism.

Finding 6. Adoption of Iranian governance by later Greek and Roman empires. Cole and Symes (2017) noted some Greek intellectuals "echoed Persian imperial decrees" to strengthen their arguments (p. 71). Later rulers such as Alexander the Great, Hellenistic kingdoms, Roman and Byzantine emperors, and Muslim caliphs will adopt the idea of Persian absolute kingship, Persian imperial model such as the satrapal system and institutions, or wish to emulate Cyrus the Great's policies (Cole & Symes, 2017; King, 2000; Noble et al., 2011). Sherman and Salisbury (2014) stated in the story of the West, "the Persian Empire marks a culmination of the first stirrings of Western civilization in the ancient Middle East" followed by the Greeks (p. 36).

Finding 7. The origins of King Arthur and his knights. With respect to Arthurian legends, King (2000) and Kishlansky et al. (2010) did not discuss Arthurian legends. Campbell (2015) stated that King Arthur's legend supported the legitimacy of later European kings (p. 200). Kidner et al. (2014), McKay et al. (2014), Sherman and Salisbury (2014), and Spielvogel (2015) described Arthurian legends as providing a powerful model of chivalric European kingship or brave knighthood. Kidner et al. (2014) and Spielvogel (2015) said a fifth or sixth century king of the Britons served as a model for the origins of King Arthur's tales. Campbell (2015), McKay et al. (2014), Noble et al. (2014), Perry et al. (2011), and Sherman and Salisbury (2014) characterized them as Anglo-Saxon (Germanic), Roman, and/or Celtic.

Finding 8. The relationship of Iranian Alans with the ruling Visigoths and Merovingians. None of the eleven surveyed textbooks covered the role of Alans in ancient European politics.

Human rights as a unique Western trait. The researcher looked up the words human rights, Cyrus, Cyrus Cylinder, Code of Chivalry, and equality for the following description based on expert opinion.

Many scholars and institutions consider the 539 BCE proclamation by the Persian king Cyrus the Great, known as the Cyrus Cylinder, as the first human rights decree (United Nations, 2008; The British Museum, 2016; IHF America, 2012; United for Human Rights, 2016; Foltz, 2016; Time-Life, 1995). A replica of the Cyrus Cylinder is at the United Nations and serves as a symbol of tolerance and freedom (IHF America, 2012; Razmjou, 2005). Its provisions parallel the first four Articles of the Universal Declaration of Human Rights (United for Human Rights, 2016). The Iranian policy to return Babylonian captives such as the Jews to their homeland, as set forth by Cyrus the Great, was unique and a reversal of policies by the Assyrian and Babylonian kings (The British Museum, 2016; IHF America, 2012; Boyce, 1987; Mallowan, 2003; Time-Life, 1995). The concept of human rights spread from ancient Persia to Greece and eventually Rome from which the idea of "natural law" emerged (United for Human Rights, 2016, p. 1). The Athenians based their democracy on exclusion with penalty for dissent while the contemporary Persian Empire was socio-politically and religiously inclusive (Meadows, 2005, p. 181). The Achaemenid Persian Empire lasted for some 220 years due to "rather gentle, farsighted and altogether successful policy," and the Jewish communities experienced prosperity and creativity (Wisesehöfer, 2006; Foltz, 2016).

The Iranian Parthian Empire (247 BCE – 224 CE) continued the Iranian traditions by protecting the persecuted minorities of the Roman empire such as the Christians in providing religious freedom and opportunities for economic and social advances (Wisesehöfer, 2006; Foltz, 2016). The knights of the Arthurian tales, which are influenced by Iranian traditions (Littleton & Malcor, 2000), lived by a code of chivalry consisting of courage, honor, and respect. These knights were equal to each other and were willing to die for worthy causes such as Truth and love (England, 2005, p. 6).

Cosentino (2004) claimed that during the fifth and the sixth century *barbarization* of Roman army, Iranians were among non-Roman recruits (p. 245). According to Nickel (1973-1974), the best equestrians in antiquity were the Scythians, who lived near the Black Sea neighboring the Greeks. Herodotus called the children of the Scythian and Amazonian union, the Sauromatae. During the Roman era, the Sarmatians entered Europe "as the first heavy armored cavalry" (Nickel, 1973-1974, p. 150) and influenced Roman adoption of heavy armored cavalry (Brzezinski & Mielczarek, 2002). The Roman army took on Alanic and Sarmatian style lances given many Roman units included Sarmatian warriors (Sidnell, 2006, p. 262). Ancient accounts noted Sarmatian ingenuity in making scales and the wealthiest Sarmatians wearing chain mail and having armor for their horses (Sidnell, 2006, p. 264). By 4th century, the Alans—cousins to Scythians and Sarmatians—entered the scene as allies of Germanic Goths, who defeated the Romans at Adrianople in 378 (Nickel, 1973-1974; Brzezinski & Mielczarek, 2002). This event "heralded the dominance of the heavy armored horseman on the medieval battlefield" (Nickel, 1973-1974, p. 150). These heavy armored cavalry brought segmented helmets and scale body armor with them. They even covered their horses with scales (Nickel,

1973-1974, p. 151). Alans settled in Spain, France, and Northern Africa (Nickel, 1973-1974; Brzezinski & Mielczarek, 2002). Their settlements in Spain and France bear their name, respectively—Catalonia (Goth-Alania) and Alençon. Chivalry developed when the Germanic Normans "came to northern France and took up the horsemanship of the Alanic gentry" (Nickel, 1973-1974, p. 150). The victory at the battle of Hastings in 1066 was partially indebted to the historical and famous Iranian tactic known as the *Parthian Shot* used by the left wing of the Norman cavalry under the direction of Alan the Red, the Count of Brittany (Nickel, 1973-1974, pp. 150-151). In 2nd century, the Romans sent the Iazyges, a branch of the Sarmatians, to fight the Picts in northern Britain. They settled in Hungary as well as what is now modern Ribchester in Lancanshire, where several hundred years later, their descendants were still listed as Sarmatians (Nickel, 1973-1974, p. 151). Iranians such as the Scythians, Sarmatians, and the Alans "possessed a highly developed epic tradition" and the great western European heroic epics such as the Arthurian legends revolved around fifth century heroes—at a time of the major influx of the Iranian nomads into Western Europe (Nickel, 1973-1974, p. 152).

The researcher used the most commonly shared elements of this broad description from among experts to analyze Iranians in connection with human rights as a unique Western trait in the surveyed college history textbooks.

Finding 1. Cyrus the Great or the Persians viewed as a savior or Messiah. With the exception of Campbell's (2015) silence on the topic, the other ten textbooks in the study claimed that Cyrus the Great was a savior or Messiah, who freed those enslaved by previous empires such as Assyrians and Babylonians, or discussed the Persians having reversed previous empires' policy of terror to free enslaved peoples in restoring law and order to the region.

Finding 2. The Cyrus Cylinder as a human rights decree. Cole and Symes (2017) referred to the Cyrus Cylinder as a propaganda "inscription honoring Cyrus" on conquering Babylon (p. 520). Cole and Symes (2017) even asserted that one could not translate the Greek word for freedom (*eleutheria*) into any ancient Near Eastern language (p. 85). McKay et al. (2014) called the Cyrus Cylinder "a text written in cuneiform" by an unknown author that presented Cyrus as a divinely chosen savior whose conquest of Babylon benefited the peoples (pp. 52-53). Spielvogel (2015) claimed the Cyrus Cylinder was a propaganda decree in representing the Persians as less cruel and more tolerant (p. 43).

Finding 3. Athenian democracy versus Persian Empire. In comparing law and order between Athenian democracy and Persian imperialism, all eleven surveyed textbooks noted that Athenian democracy benefited Athenian male citizens (about 20% of the city's population), sanctioned slavery, promoted the rule of the elites, or was unattractive to other Greek cities because it was costly. All eleven textbooks in the study claimed that the Greeks admired the Persian Empire for its political stability and trained bureaucracy compared to their own, fostering peace through tolerance and good treatment of peoples across the empire, creating a multicultural political unity, and being law-abiding.

Finding 4. Parthian Empire and minorities such as the Jewish and Christian communities. None of the surveyed textbooks discussed the Parthian Empire and the treatment of minorities.

Finding 5. Origins of Code of Chivalry. Although all eleven surveyed textbooks referred to the Code of Chivalry that flourished in Europe by 12th century as demonstrated by the Arthurian tales, none mentioned Iran's positioning with respect to its development even though many of the textbooks pointed to France (ancient Gaul) as place of origin.

Democracy as a unique Western trait. The researcher looked up the words democracy and Darius for the following description based on expert opinion.

Greece experienced an era of growth, prosperity, and confidence after victories at the Greco-Persian Wars (499-449 BCE). For Athens, its young democracy changed considerably (Raaflaub, 1999) as it came to maturity while its citizens experienced an extraordinary cultural achievement (Kagan, 2003; Briant, 2002). The events of the Greco-Persian Wars became part of the Hellenic national legend and a lasting experience in the psyche of Western traditions (Time-Life, 1995).

In 499 BCE, after the Persians quashed the initial outbreak of the Greco-Persian Wars known as the Ionian Revolt, King Darius the Great ordered two amazing and constructing reforms. First, he pressured Greeks to settle their differences in a judicial manner rather than their traditional border-raiding tactics. Second, he replaced the unpopular Ionian tyrants with democracies (Burn, 2003, pp. 311-312). Finally, with the intrusion of the Persian Empire starting mid-sixth century BCE, the hybrid Athenian democracy experienced a crucial transition as the Greek world began forming its own style of imperialism (Raaflaub, 1999, p. 148). Raaflaub et al (2007) believed the earliest use of the word *demokratia* (people power) took place probably after 420 BCE reflecting both institutional and linguistic changes due to military prowess and political order experienced after the Greco-Persian Wars (p. 162).

Although democracy is seen by many as a Greek phenomenon (Raaflaub, Ober, & Wallace, 2007), the Athenian democracy was not 100% direct participation. It did not entail the modern concepts of representation, separation of power, and the rule of law (Samiei, 2014). Further, there is evidence that Athenians did not invent the idea of democracy (Samiei, 2014; Zikakou, 2015). One may observe this type of government among non-Greeks such as Phoenicians (Samiei, 2014). Greek historian Herodotus reported that by 522 BCE, the Persians debated different forms of government, including democracy, and this was "long before the Athenians themselves converted to democracy with Cleisthenes' reforms, in 509 BCE" (Sissa, 2012, p. 233). Although Raaflaub et al. (2007) recognized that experts disagree on the origins of democracy in Greece, they are of the view that it was with Cleisthenes immediately after 508/7 BCE. With this in mind, Sissa (2012) suggested the invention of democracy appeared "in the mind of a Persian aristocrat" about fifteen years before Cleisthenes' reforms (p. 261). According to Abbott (1898), the co-called *Persian Debate* as described by Herodotus showed that it "was a story current among the Greeks of Ionia, but rejected by some of them" (p. 247). Both Thompson (1996) and Mann (1999) noted that critics such as Raaflaub et al. (2007) do not have a firm ground on rejecting the reporting of a so-called Persian Debate by Herodotus as fabrication or misinformation, because Herodotus specifically addressed his skeptical contemporaries.

The researcher used the most commonly shared elements of this broad description from among experts to analyze Iranians in connection with democracy as a unique Western trait in the surveyed college history textbooks.

Finding 1. Athenian democracy and the Greco-Persian Wars. Nine out of eleven textbooks in the study viewed the Greco-Persian Wars (499-449 BCE) as decisive, defining, and key to the rising importance of Athens in strengthening its democracy and ultimate transformation to a regional empire (Campbell, 2015; Cole & Symes, 2017; Kidner et al., 2014; Kishlansky et al., 2010; McKay et al., 2014; Noble et al., 2011; Perry et al., 2016; Sherman &

Salisbury, 2014; Spielvogel, 2015). Hunt et al. (2017), Perry et al. (2016), and Spielvogel (2015) attributed the Greek Golden or Classical Age (478-431 BCE) during which Greek innovations in architecture, arts, and theater boomed to the Greco-Persian Wars (499-449 BCE).

Finding 2. Darius and the Ionian Revolt. None of the surveyed textbooks discussed how the Persian king Darius the Great authorized democratic governments for Greek cities in Asia Minor after the Ionian Revolt (499-493 BCE) or the Persian Debate on different types of government including democracy as described by Herodotus.

Finding 3. The origins of democracy. Nine out of eleven surveyed textbooks claimed or suggested the birth of democracy was in Athens or was Greek in origin (Campbell, 2015; Cole & Symes, 2017; Hunt et al., 2017; Kidner et al., 2017; King, 2000; McKay et al., 2014; Noble et al., 2011; Sherman & Salisbury, 2014; Spielvogel, 2015). Hunt et al. (2017), Noble et al. (2011), Perry et al. (2016), and Sherman and Salisbury (2014) explained that Solon's political changes around 594 BCE would set the foundation for a democracy in Athens. Ten out of eleven surveyed textbooks considered the reforms by Athenian politician Cleisthenes around 508-507 BCE as the catalyst for establishing a democracy (Cole & Symes, 2017; Hunt et al., 2017; Kidner et al., 2017; King, 2000; Kishlansky et al., 2010; McKay et al., 2014; Noble et al., 2011; Perry et al., 2016; Sherman & Salisbury, 2014; Spielvogel, 2015).

Individualism as a unique Western trait. The researcher looked up the words individualism, free will, choice, Zoroaster, and Zoroastrianism for the following description based on expert opinion.

According to Huntington (1996), individualism refers to "the right of individual choice" (p. 3). Duchesne (2011) regarded the Western unique trait of individualism as "the attainment of honorable prestige through the performance of heroic deeds" (p. x). Ethical dualism—attributed to Iranian Zoroastrianism—teaches that men and women must choose between good and evil in life (Clark, 2001, p. 9; Boyce, 1987, p. 20; Nanavutty, 1999, pp. 35-36) since the increase or decrease of evil in the world is based on individual's free will to follow or reject the primordial Lie (evil) (Clark, 2001, p. 9). Individuals have inborn faculties such as physical bodies, awakened conscience, and directive intelligence to discriminate between good and evil (Nanavutty, 1999, p. 36).

One notes individual choice and heroism in Iranian national history. Frye (2004) claimed the eastern Iranian Kayanian heroic cycle served as the main source for all Iranian epics (p. 38). In Old Iranian, Kay (Kai, Kavi) means ruler or prince (Nanavutty, 1999), and Kayanian tradition refers to ancient mythical Iranian kings (Wisesehöfer, 2006; Nanavutty, 1999). The Arthurian legends are an example of Western heroic traditions. Littleton and Malcor (2000) proposed the Arthurian tales are Iranian in origin. One of the earliest figures among King Arthur's knight is Sir Kay (Cai, Cei) whose name may be derived from an ancient Iranian warrior named Kay (Kai) (Littleton & Malcor, 2000).

The researcher used the most commonly shared elements of this broad description from among experts to analyze Iranians in connection with individualism as a unique Western trait in the surveyed college history textbooks.

Finding 1. Ethical dualism of Zoroastrianism including free will or choice. Campbell (2015) and King (2000) did not discuss Zoroastrianism and individualism. Kishlansky et al. (2010) questioned Greek notion of freedom as not based on individualism, rather a multitude of collectivities. That is, Athenian freedom was not freedom from community, but freedom in community (Kishlansky et al., 2000, p. 62). The other eight surveyed textbooks explained the role of free will, individual choices and responsibilities, moral and ethical dualism, and pursuit of spiritual purity in the teachings of Zoroastrianism. Hunt et al. (2017), Kidner et al. (2014), Sherman and Salisbury (2014), and Spielvogel (2015) claimed these Zoroastrian views regarding human behavior and role influenced others. Cole and Symes (2017) and McKay et al. (2014) called Zoroaster's concepts new. Sherman and Salisbury (2014) stated Zoroaster was the first prophet whose ideas spread across a large political empire.

Finding 2. Heroism in Iranian national history and Arthurian tales. King (2000) claimed the Iranian sun god Mithras was a favorite among Romans because, based on its Zoroastrian roots, heroic Mithras fought evil. With respect to Arthurian legends, King (2000) and Kishlansky et al. (2010) did not discuss Arthurian legends. Campbell (2015), Cole and Symes (2017), Hunt et al. (2017), Kidner et al. (2014), McKay et al. (2014), Noble et al. (2014), Perry et al. (2011), and Sherman and Salisbury (2014) described the popularity of Arthurian legends based on ancient king of Britain due to its promotion of heroic deeds and choices, chivalry, or ideal courtiers. Kidner et al. (2014) and Spielvogel (2015) said a fifth or sixth century king of the Britons served as a model for the origins of King Arthur's stories. Campbell (2015), McKay et al. (2014), Noble et al. (2014), Perry et al. (2011), and Sherman and Salisbury (2014) characterized them as Anglo-Saxon (Germanic), Roman, and/or Celtic.

Christianity as a unique Western trait. The researcher looked up the words Zoroaster, Zoroastrianism, Mithraism, Manichaeism, and Magi for the following description based on expert opinion.

> One of the most significant encounters in the history of religions is the encounter of ancient Iranians and Israelites (Foltz, 2016). Later religions such as Christianity and Islam adopted concepts from Iranian religion known as Zoroastrianism such as heaven

and hell, angels and demons, the Devil, Resurrection, and the Last Judgment along with a Messiah figure following an apocalyptic battle between good and evil (Foltz, 2016; Clark, 2001; Russell, 1992). Even the word paradise originates from a Persian word and idea meaning an enclosed garden or park (Clark, 2001, p. 154; Time-Life, 1995, p. 62). These notions were absent from ancient Israelite beliefs. The Israelites embraced these ideas from Iranian priests known as the Magi (Foltz, 2016). In addition to the Judeo-Christian-Islamic trinity's adoption of these Iranian leading religious doctrines, many Gnostic faiths and northern Buddhism were influenced by Zoroastrianism as well (Boyce, 1987, p. 1).

Boyce (1987) considered Zoroastrianism as "the oldest of the revealed creedal religions" and one that "has probably had more influence on mankind, directly or indirectly, than any other single faith" (p. 1). Muesse (2013) claimed, "Zoroastrianism may well have had the greatest impact of any single religion in the world," because of its demand for moral responsibility and a belief in a final destiny for the cosmos (p. 27). Waterhouse (1934/2006) felt that Christian heritage through Judaism was enriched by Zoroastrianism given its monotheistic teachings based on ethics (p. 9). One may not categorize pre-exilic Judaism as monotheistic since there is evidence that they acknowledged multiple deities at the time (Clark, 2001). Clark (2003) stated that ancient Iranian prophet and philosopher Zoroaster "heralded the beginnings of Western civilization" (p. 1). Zoroastrianism is still part of the cultural fabric of the West through the domination of Judeo-Christian traditions (Clark, 2001, p. 1).

In the Old Testament, the Persian king Cyrus the Great is hailed as a Messiah and the scripture verses may be viewed as "the first imprint of that influence which

Zoroastrianism was to exert so powerfully on post-Exilic Judaism" (Boyce, 1987, p. 52). Some scholars regarded Antioch in Syria as the place of origin for the gospel; thus, Matthew may have partly focused his missionary work at the Zoroastrian community in the region (Clark, 2001, p. 156). Christianity arose after exposure to 500 years of contact with Zoroastrianism enriched Judaism. Hence, this new religion was a fusion between Semitic and Iranian beliefs (Boyce, 1987).

Frye (2004) noted Iranians influenced the Jews and Israel. It is under the Achaemenid Persian rule that the Torah became the law of Israel and some scholars date the rise of modern Judaism under Persian imperial approval from this period (Frye, 2004, p. 135). The Persian court commissioned the Jewish legal expert and worshipper of Yahweh Ezra to re-establish the temple at Jerusalem (Clark, 2001). The Persian kings sent both Ezra and Nehemiah escorted by armed men to Jerusalem to handle Jewish re-settlement (Briant, 2002). The study of the Old Testament is concerned with historical facts and importance of the Persian Empire in the history of ancient Jewish communities as well as the development of the Old Testament itself (Wisesehöfer, 2006, p. 12).

According to Dr. Shai Secunda, the most important religious book that the Jewish people focus on is the Babylonian Talmud because it defines Jewish life and beliefs (Library of Congress, 2014). Although there are two Talmuds (Babylonian versus Jersualem or Palestinian versions), the most important and dominant one is the Babylonian Talmud. The Babylonian Talmud was produced from around third century to early seventh century in ancient Babylonia which at the time was the center of power for an Iranian government—the Sasanian era (224-651). The Sasanian Persian Empire viewed Babylonia as part of its territories and called it Assuristan (Assyria) (Library of

Congress, 2014). It was not a foreign land to Iranians. It was the heart of the Iranian empire. Therefore, the creators of the Talmud produced it in the heart of the ancient Iranian empire at a place where Jewish rabbis mingled with Iranian nobility and Zoroastrian priests. Hence, Secunda's most innovative suggestion is to see the Talmud as always and invariably Iranian (Gross, 2014, p. 6). Foltz (2016) noted that many Israelites stayed "as free citizen in Persian-ruled Babylonia"—a place that became "the center of Jewish civilization" for centuries and from which the Talmudic religion was produced (p. 15).

The Iranian interference in Jerusalem appeared to have caused a schism as many Jews resisted the influence of Zoroastrianism. The Sadducees or the purists did not believe in Persian ideas such as resurrection and angels. The minority Jewish group under Iranian influences, the Pharisees, survived the fall of Jerusalem under the Roman Empire in 70 CE (Wiley, 2015). The Pharisees believed in resurrection of the just and the Messiah which were ideas of Persian origin (Forlong, 1906). Some scholars believe the name *Pharisee* means "Persian" ("Religious Systems," 1892; Forlong, 1906; Malina & Pilch, 2006; Wiley, 2015).

According to father of Christian chronography Libyan-Roman Sextus Julius Africanus (3rd c.) and Archbishop of Constantinople St. John Chrysostom (4th c.), the world first learned of the birth of Christ (the Messiah for the Jews) from the Persians (as cited by Silver, 2013, p. 178; as cited by Watefield, 2011, p. 16). The tradition that the three kings (Magi) who came to worship Christ at his birth were Persian is "old and honorable" (Waterfield, 2011, p. 16; Razmjou, 2005, p. 154). The cross of the apostle St.

Thomas, who was sent to Iranian territories and later India for preaching and converting, is also known as the Persian Cross (Brave Catholic, 2016).

Other Iranian religions Mithraism and Manichaeism—offshoots of Zoroastrianism—also influenced Christianity (Razmjou, 2005; Goucher & Walton, 2008; Littleton & Malcor, 2000). In a 1949 college paper, Dr. Martin Luther King Jr. wrote that the similarities between Mithraism and Christianity are so great that it is a challenge for any modern student to investigate (p. 2). Additionally, King Jr. (1949) noted that one might not deny that Christianity borrowed ideas from Mithraism, because "it was generally a natural and unconscious process" (p. 8).

Colpe (2004) stated that several individuals who were familiar with Platonic traditions, Greek mysteries, Iranian Zoroastrianism, and the Indo-Iranian sun god Mithra developed the Roman version of Mithraism (p. 855). Kreisberg (2012) wrote that the last pope of the cult of Mithras died in Rome in 384. Evidence indicates that the fourth century Vatican was the home of the leader of Mithraism (Kreisberg, 2012). Mithraism was so popular and widespread among Romans, including women, that a top 20th c. historian, Yale professor Michael Rostovtzeff, claimed it "might conceivably have remained the lasting religion of the Roman state if Christianity had not developed" because "the religion of the Persian empire Iranized Rome" (Rostovtzeff, 1929, p. 1). Razmjou (2005) noted that the Romans spread Mithraism across Europe as far as England.

Constantine the Great had affiliations with Mithraism. St. Ambrose, the bishop of Milan, came from an elite Roman family whose father was a Mithraist (Kreisberg, 2012). Church Fathers either attacked, or remained silent on, similarities between Mithraic and

Christian doctrines. They considered Mithraism as the most dangerous rival to Christianity—one that must be crushed for the church to survive (Laing, 1918; Boyce, 1987). Despite these efforts, "Mithraic traditions survived and even thrived in the esoteric undercurrents of Western civilization, and they do so to this day" (Ruck, Hoffman, & Celdrán, 2011, p. 25). Littleton and Malcor (2000) claimed Iranian traditions such as Mithraism profoundly influenced the concept of the Holy Grail and its legends as encountered in the King Arthur tales (p. 220 and 282).

The third century Iranian prophet Mani combined Iranian dualism of Zoroastrianism with Syriac Christianity to form an indigenous religion (Colpe, 2004). Manichaean ideas influenced early Christian Church. St. Augustine, one of greatest Christian thinkers and a Church Father, converted from Manichaeism to Christianity (Goucher & Walton, 2008, p. 90). In fourth century, many Mithraic elements survived in Roman territories after the rise of Christianity because they were incorporated into Manichaeism (Colpe, 2004, p. 857). Although Alans (Iranian stock) eventually adopted Christianity, given their domain in Europe was under the influence of Eastern elements, they might have converted to a form of Christianity influenced by Manichaeism (Littleton & Malcor, 2000).

A Scythian (Iranian stock) monk Dionysius Exiguus invented Anno Domini (AD)—the style of counting the years. He was part of a larger Scythian group of monks, who were influential in early Christian theological disputes between 4th and 6th centuries. Dionysius Exiguus wrote the Collectio Dinoysiana and many other canons of councils and synods (Rothwangl, 2016, p. 1). In the spread of Christianity across Eastern Asia, Sogdians (Iranian stock) played a key part (Foltz, 2016). In Europe, Littleton and

Malcor (2000) cited many members of Alan (Iranian stock) families in Gaul who were bishops as early as 6th century after the collapse of the Western Roman Empire. Starting in fifth century Gaul, there was an unbroken line of Alan rules both in the church and among the nobility (Littleton & Malcor, 2000, pp. 38-39).

The researcher used the most commonly shared elements of this broad description from among experts to analyze Iranians in connection with Christianity as a unique Western trait in the surveyed college history textbooks.

Finding 1. The impact of Zoroastrian concepts on Judeo-Christianity. These concepts include heaven (paradise) and hell, angels and demons, the Devil, Resurrection, and the Last Judgment along with a Messiah figure following an apocalyptic battle between good and evil. Cole and Symes (2017) asserted that both Zoroastrianism and Judaism were the West's most enduring and influential religions (p. 32). Four textbooks in the study claimed Zoroastrian ideas such as God/Satan, angels/demons, Judgment Day, Messiah, and ethical behavior influenced later religions (Cole & Symes, 2017; Hunt et al., 2017, Kidner et al., 2014; McKay et al., 2014). Six surveyed textbooks noted that Zoroastrian ideas influenced Christianity (Cole & Symes, 2017; Kidner et al., 2014; King, 2000; McKay et al., 2014; Sherman & Salisbury, 2014; Spielvogel, 2015). Cole and Symes (2017) and Spielvogel (2015) presented Zoroastrianism and Judaism as similar or parallel in some of their ideas while Hunt et al. (2017), King (2000), Perry et al. (2016), and Sherman and Salisbury (2014) argued that Zoroastrianism influenced Judaism. Campbell (2015), McKay et al. (2014), and Noble et al. (2011) stated Mesopotamian culture influenced Judaism.

Finding 2. Origins of Monotheism, moral responsibility, and final destiny of the cosmos. Campbell (2015) and Perry et al. (2016) pointed to Egypt for the origins of monotheism that influenced Judaism. Cole and Symes (2017), Hunt et al. (2017), and McKay et al. (2014) named the Hebrews as developers of monotheism. Cole and Symes (2017), Hunt et al. (2017), King (2000), and Sherman and Salisbury (2014) said Zoroaster formulated moral dualism. King (2000) also claimed that moral dualism, which was dependent on monotheism, developed independently across the world. Spielvogel (2015) called both Zoroastrianism and Judaism monotheistic religions.

Finding 3. Ezra, Nehemiah, and Pharisees. Kidner et al. (2014) recalled Ester as a Jewish woman in the Persian court. Kidner et al. (2014), Kishlansky et al. (2010), and Noble et al. (2011) referred to Nehemiah, governor of Judah, and Ezra, who presided over completion and adoption of the Torah, as important figures in transformation of Judaism. However, only Kidner et al. (2014) identified Nehemiah and Ezra with the Persian Court. Eight textbooks covered the radical and transformative role of the Pharisee Jews in the development of modern Judaism including their adoption of ideas such as life after death, Judgment Day, and Messiah (Campbell, 2015; Cole & Symes, 2017; Kidner et al., 2014; King, 2000; Kishlansky et al., 2010; Noble et al., 2010; Perry et al., 2016; Sherman & Salisbury, 2014). However, only King (2000) and Perry et al. (2016) noted that the Pharisees were influenced by the Persians or Zoroastrianism while Kidner et al. (2014) asserted that they were influenced by foreign views. King (2000) and Noble et al. (2011) translated *Pharisee* as *separated* while Kishlansky et al. (2010) translated it as *non-Jews*. Campbell (2015), Cole and Symes (2017), and Noble et al. (2011) stated that Jesus either followed the Pharisee teachings or was regarded by his contemporaries as a Pharisee. Kidner et al. (2014) noted that St. Paul was a Pharisee.

Finding 4. Birth of Christ and the Magi. Three of eleven surveyed textbooks discussed the Magi and baby Jesus, but only Noble et al. (2011) identified them as wise men from the East.

Finding 5. St. Ambrose, St. Augustine, and St. Thomas. Six surveyed textbooks referred to St. Augustine's conversion to Christianity (Cole & Symes, 2017; King, 2000; Kishlansky et al., 2010; McKay et al., 2014; Noble et al., 2011; Perry et al., 2016), but only three specified that it was from Persian Manichaeism. McKay et al. (2014) did not identify the religion from which St. Ambrose converted to Christianity.

Finding 6. The impact of Mithraism and Manichaeism on Christianity. King (2000), Perry et al. (2016), and Spielvogel (2015) claimed Persian Mithraism affected Christianity while Cole and Symes (2017) in making a similar suggestion did not identify the origins of Mithraism. Cole and Symes (2017) and King (2000) stated that Persian Manichaeism influenced Christianity while Kidner et al. (2014) stated the two shared certain aspects. King (2000), Noble et al. (2011), Perry et al. (2016), and Sherman and Salisbury (2014) said Persian Zoroastrianism or Manichaeism influenced the medieval European movements of Cathars and Albigensians treated as heretics by the Church.

Finding 7. Vatican and Mithraism. None of the textbooks in the study mentioned the Vatican and Mithraism relation.

Finding 8. Origins of the Holy Grail tales. Campbell (2015), Cole and Symes (2017), and Hunt et al. (2017) covered the relation between the Holy Grail and Arthurian tales without further discussions on origins.

Finding 9. Scythian monks. None of the textbooks in the study mentioned the Scythian Christian monks.

Finding 10. Christian Alans in ancient Europe. None of the surveyed textbooks mentioned the Christian Alans in Europe.

Discrepancies during Data Collection

The following are some discrepancies that the researcher encountered during data collection. First, the researcher relied on the searching mechanism in selected electronic textbooks and the Index of printed textbooks. Second, in searching the surveyed textbooks on Themes 1 and 2, some did not have certain words of interest in the Index or Glossary. For example, Indo-European was not in Kishlansky et al.'s (2010) Index; however, the word Semites was in the Index. By looking up Semites on pages noted in Kishlansky et al.'s (2010) Index, the researcher was able to find reference to Indo-Europeans. A third discrepancy involved spelling of words. Sometimes surveyed textbooks spelled words of interest differently. For example, Campbell (2015) and Perry et al. (2016) spelled Mitanni as Mittani. Fourth, the researcher also noticed that at times information showed up in the surveyed textbooks later than where a reader would have anticipated. For example, in King (2000) and Sherman and Salisbury (2014), the connection between Persia and Iran came up in later chapters dealing with modern era rather than in the Age of Antiquity section of textbooks. Finally, the researcher noted errors in information. For example, King (2000) confused two Persian kings Cyrus I (grandfather) with Cyrus II (grandson).

Summary

The purpose of this qualitative case study was to discover how a selected sample of college history textbooks position Iran and Iranians in the origins of Western Civilization. In this chapter, the researcher organized the findings according to the research questions and thematic approach. The researcher provided both expert opinion and selected textbook content for each theme in support of the findings. As is typical with qualitative research, numerous quotations were also included in this report. These direct quotes should strengthen the readers' confidence on the accuracy of data collection. Appendix D is a quick reference to the following summary.

In defining Iran under Theme 1, more than half of the surveyed textbooks claimed there were no Aryan people or Aryan race. Two surveyed textbooks did not mention Aryans. Only one textbook in the study noted that the word Iran derived from Aryan. Majority of the textbooks associated Aryan with 20th century Nazism in Germany. None of the surveyed textbooks covered Greater Iran. More than half the textbooks equated Persia with Iran without any explanation.

In defining Iranians under Theme 1, only one surveyed textbook stated that the Medes were Iranian and one noted that the Medes and Persians were Aryans. Seven out of eleven textbooks in the study stated that the Medes and Persians were Indo-Europeans. Only four of the surveyed textbooks referred to the presence of the Persians in Europe. None of the surveyed textbooks discussed the numerous Iranian tribes.

In defining Iranian languages under Theme 1, only two textbooks in the study specifically noted that Iranian language was Indo-European. Two surveyed textbooks covered Indo-European languages but did not include the Iranian branch. Half of the surveyed textbooks labeled either Persian and/or Median as Indo-European. None of the surveyed textbooks covered the numerous Iranian languages.

With respect to roots and origins of Iranians under Theme 2, none of the surveyed textbooks covered the proto-Indo-Iranians or ancient home of the Iranian branch. Seven out of eleven textbooks in the study claimed that Indo-Europeans settled in Iran by second millennium BCE.

In covering 27 selected Iranian tribes inhabiting ancient Asia (19/27) and Europe (8/27) under Themes 3 and 4, none of the textbooks in the study covered or identified 11 of 19 Asiatic tribes while they mentioned six of 19 Asiatic tribes without identifying them as Iranian. The remaining two Asiatic tribes—Medes and Persians—received the most attention in the surveyed textbooks. Two of the selected textbooks identified the Medes as Iranian, one identified them as Indo-European Aryans of Iran, and seven called them Indo-Europeans. One out of eleven surveyed textbooks labeled the Persians as Indo-European Aryans of Iran, five called them Indo-Europeans, and one identified them as Iranian. None of the surveyed textbooks covered four of the eight European tribes (Aorsi, Cimmerian, Iazyges/Jasz, and Roxolani). The textbooks in the study barely covered the remaining four European tribes (Alan, Ossetian, Saka/Scythian, and Sarmatian/Sauromatian) and did not identify them as Iranian.

With respect to Greek philosophy under Theme 5, none of the surveyed textbooks stated that Greek philosophy flourished under the Persian Empire even though all eleven stated that its birth was in 6th century BCE Ionian city of Miletus in Asia Minor. Four textbooks claimed that 6th century BCE Ionian Greeks were under Persian Empire. Most textbooks in the study described the influences of Egypt, Babylonia, Near Eastern, and Mesopotamia on Greek philosophy. A few noted Greco-Persian Wars influenced the birth of Classical Age in Greece. Majority of surveyed textbooks dated Zoroaster to 6th century BCE rather than the second millennium BCE. Ten textbooks in the study covered new concepts under Zoroastrianism such as cosmic dualism, but did not connect them to Greek philosophy. Almost all surveyed textbooks covered Zoroaster's teachings including free will, personal responsibility, freedom to choose, morality, and ethical thinking. Seven of eleven selected textbooks defined Magi as Zoroastrian or Iranian priests/wisemen but without connections to Greek philosophy. Some of the textbooks in the study named a few Greek intellectuals such as Herodotus and Xenophon in relation to their knowledge and writings about Iran, but in no relation to Greek philosophy. Only two textbooks in the study discussed Iran's role in saving exiled Neoplatonic Academy. Ten surveyed textbooks attributed the ultimate translations, preservation, and transmission of Greek knowledge to the West to medieval Arabs or Muslims. Only one textbook in the study credited Iran for sheltering Greek knowledge.

With respect to law and order under Theme 5, six of eleven surveyed textbooks called Cyrus a lawgiver, savior, and restorer. Four surveyed textbooks said Cyrus was an unusual ruler and/or reversed oppressive policies. Five of eleven textbooks in the study labeled Darius a good administrator and lawgiver. All surveyed textbooks described the Persian Empire as effective, efficient, diverse and politically united, tolerant, and managed with law and order to promote peace and prosperity. Six surveyed textbooks noted that ancient peoples viewed Persian kings as the Great King or King of Kings. Eight textbooks in the study covered Iran's satrapal system in promoting law and order. Three textbooks in the study stated that later rulers and empires adopted the ancient Iranian governance. Only one surveyed textbook stated that the Persian Empire was the pinnacle of the first awakenings of Western Civilization followed by the Greeks. None of the surveyed textbooks mentioned the law of the Medes and Persians, Medism under Greek laws, Iranian aspect of Arthurian tales, and Iranian Alans in governance of ancient Europe.

With respect to human rights under Theme 5, ten surveyed textbooks claimed Cyrus or the Persians saved people from terror and enslavement. Tree selected textbooks mentioned the Cyrus Cylinder, but none associated it with human rights. All textbooks in the study discussed how Athenian democracy only benefited a small percentage of the city population while promoting slavery and elitism. All textbooks in the study covered the Persian Empire's multicultural, diverse, tolerant, and politically stable government. None of the surveyed textbooks discussed the minorities under Iranian Parthian dynasty. None of the surveyed textbooks attributed the Arthurian Code of Chivalry to Iranians.

With respect to democracy under Theme 5, nine of eleven surveyed textbooks claimed the experience of the Greco-Persian Wars strengthened Athens' democracy. A few stated that the Greco-Persian Wars launched the Classical Age or the Golden Age in Greece. Nine textbooks in the study attributed the birth of democracy in Athens or Greece. Almost all surveyed textbooks credited the reforms of Cleisthenes around 508-507 BCE for the launch of democracy in Athens. None of the surveyed textbooks covered the Persian Debate about democracy that took place before the reforms of Cleisthenes or the role of Darius regarding democracy in Ionia (Asia Minor).

With respect to individualism under Theme 5, eight of eleven selected textbooks described free will, individualism, choices and personal responsibility, and moral and ethical dualism in Zoroastrianism teachings. Four textbooks in the study claimed Zoroastrian views on human behavior influenced others while two textbooks stated that Zoroastrian concepts were new. One textbook in the study claimed that Zoroaster was the first prophet whose teachings spread across a major empire. One textbook in the study mentioned Iranian Mithraic popularity among the Romans because of its heroic teachings, but none discussed Arthurian heroism and Iranian origins.

With respect to Christianity under Theme 5, four selected textbooks claimed Zoroastrianism influenced others, six textbooks said it influenced Christianity, and four discussed its influences on Judaism. Four textbooks in the study stated that Zoroaster formulated moral dualism. None of the surveyed textbooks attributed origins of monotheism or Jewish monotheism to Zoroastrianism. Only one surveyed textbook identified Ezra and Nehemiah as representatives from the Persian court. Two textbooks in the study claimed the Persians influenced the Jewish Pharisees but did not translate Pharisee as Persian. Three textbooks in the study noted that St. Augustine converted from Manichaeism to Christianity while none associated St. Ambrose or St. Thomas to Iranian religions. Four textbooks in the study noted that Iranian Mithraism and Manichaeism affected Christianity. Four out of eleven surveyed textbooks claimed Zoroastrianism or Manichaeism influenced the Cathars and Albigensians in Europe. None of the surveyed textbooks identified the Magi visiting baby Jesus as Iranian, and none covered any connections between the Vatican and Mithraism, Scythian monks and Christianity, the role of Iranian Alans and Christianity in Europe, or Iranians and the Holy Grail.

CHAPTER 5

CONCLUSIONS

The purpose of this qualitative case study was to explore how a selected sample of college-level history textbooks place Iran and Iranians in the origins of Western Civilization. The researcher believed the study would contribute to knowledge base and practical application. That is, educators and students would note there is more to the origins of Western Civilization than a limited focus on Judeo-Christian-Greco-Roman narrative (Parcel & Taylor, 2015; Arnn, 2014, p. 1; Le Gates, 2001, p. 19; p. 6; Papper, 1995, p. 131). Therefore, educators and authors of history books would properly position Iran in the origins of Western Civilization, which in turn would address the pro-world history advocates' challenging the relevancy of teaching Western Civilization (Ricketts et al., 2011). The conclusions from this study follow the research questions and the findings. The researcher will finalize this discussion with some recommendations and a final reflection on this study.

Iranians are members of the Indo-European family and inhabitants of Asia and Europe since the Age of Antiquity. Thus, previous theories noted in the literature review such as Orientalism and Eurocentrism (Dabashi, 2015; Daryaee, 2005; Shariati, 2010), nativism (Morgan, 2008), or bias against Middle Eastern peoples (Brockway, 2007) do not provide sufficient explanation as to the marginalization, misrepresentation (Anvarinejad, 2007; Foltz, 2016; KPFA, 2014; Morgan & Walker, 2008; Vahdati, 2014), and omission of (Bachrach, 1973; Daragahi, 2010; Kincheloe, 2004) Iran's positioning in the history of Western Civilization. In seeking to understand this phenomenon, the researcher focused on the positioning of Iran and Iranians in the origins of Western Civilization.

Interpretation of Findings

This study focused on terminology and definition, roots and ancestry, and cultural characteristics. The study attempted to discover how Western Civilization textbooks define Iran, Iranians, and Iranian languages; explain the roots and origins of Iranians; cover Iranian peoples in the Age of Antiquity; teach about Iranian peoples in Europe during the Age of Antiquity; and discuss Iranian attributes in Europe during the Age of Antiquity.

This study found that the sampled selection of college textbooks overwhelmingly ill-defined, misrepresented, marginalized, or omitted the terms Iran, Iranians, and Iranian languages. For example, more than half of the surveyed textbooks claimed that an Aryan race or Aryan people were mythical while majority of the surveyed textbooks argued that Aryan was a modern racist notion propagated by 20th century Nazi Germany. None of the surveyed textbooks explained the relationship between Persia/Persian and Iran/Iranian. With the exception of the Medes and the Persians, the surveyed textbooks did not identify the other tribes of Iranian stock. The surveyed textbooks did not cover the scope and size of a Greater Iran or Iranian languages. Most of the surveyed textbooks did not list Iranian languages as Indo-European or, in some cases, they only acknowledged certain Iranian languages such as Persian or Median as Indo-European.

This study found that the sampled selection of textbooks overwhelmingly omitted, blurred, marginalized, or misrepresented the presentation of Iranian origins. Most of the surveyed textbooks did not cover origins or migrations of the Iranian branch of the Indo-Europeans as they spread across ancient Asia and Europe. None of the surveyed textbooks covered the ancient Iranian homeland.

This study found the surveyed textbooks overwhelmingly omitted, blurred, marginalized, or misrepresented the two-pronged positioning of Iran in the origins of Western Civilization—that is, the sampled selection of textbooks did not demonstrate that many Iranian tribes inhabited Asia and Europe and were part of the development of Asiatic and European civilizations. Iranians did not just contribute to Western Civilization as many other peoples may have had through the ages. Rather, Iranians as ancient inhabitants of Europe are part of the ancestral makeup of the West. None of the surveyed textbooks showed this critical paradigm as they promoted the inaccurate and incomplete Judeo-Christian-Greco-Roman narrative (Parcel & Taylor, 2015; Arnn, 2014; Le Gates, 2001; Papper, 1995).

Not only did the surveyed textbooks omit or not properly identify European Iranians as Iranians, but they marginalized the ones that were briefly covered. For example, the surveyed textbooks overwhelmingly ignored the role of Scythians, Sarmatians, and Alans in the conquest, settlement, and border patrol and protection of Europe. Iranian tribes such as Alans long resided in Gaul, Italy, Spain, and Africa (as cited by Bachrach, 1973, p. vii; Brzezinski & Mielczarek, 2002). Yet, none of the surveyed textbooks mentioned the position of Iranian tribes with respect to events surrounding the Greeks, Celts, Romans, or Germanic tribes as the battle ensued over centuries for the control of European territories.

This study found that the sampled selection of textbooks overwhelmingly misappropriated, omitted, or marginalized the positioning of Iran and Iranians in shaping and preserving Greek philosophy. For example, majority of the surveyed textbooks misdated the Iranian philosopher and religious reformist Zoroaster by 600-800 years—that is, placing him in the first millennium BCE rather than second millennium BCE. This is significant given many of the surveyed textbooks also claimed that Greek philosophers and Judaic-Christian-Islamic trilogy adopted certain Zoroastrian concepts such as cosmic dualism of good versus evil. Grossly misdating Zoroaster while claiming some of his teachings were original and influential are contradictory and incoherent. Additionally, none of the surveyed textbooks discussed any relation between Greek philosophers and Iranian thinking such as the role of the Magi or views of Greek thinkers about Iranian philosophy. Only a couple of surveyed textbooks credited Iran's preservation of Greek philosophy after Roman Emperor Justinian shut down the Neoplatonic Academy.

This study concluded that all of the surveyed textbooks framed Iran's historical positioning with respect to law and order as confined to some 200-year time capsule—namely, the era of the Achaemenid Persian Empire (550-330 BCE). Majority of the surveyed textbooks covered the Achaemenid Persian Empire's significance and role regarding law and order. However, they omitted its influences on the Greeks such as Medism or laws of the Medes and the Persians. Further, the surveyed textbooks virtually abandon their emphasis on Iranian law and order during the Age of Antiquity after the Achaemenids even though other Iranian governments (Parthian and Sasanian) arose post Hellenistic period from the third century BCE to seventh century CE (some 900 years). Even though a few surveyed textbooks mentioned that Iranian governance was copied or adopted by later empires such as Alexander the Great and the Byzantine emperors, this concept is not developed further in the surveyed textbooks so that students can see where and how Iranian administrative setup were used as the West developed. This is an example of abortive historical teachings in textbooks about Iran's positioning in the origins of Western Civilization. None of the surveyed textbooks attributed the law and order under Arthurian legends to Iranians or covered the role of Iranian Alans in ancient European political setup.

This study discovered that the textbooks in the study overwhelmingly omitted or presented the Cyrus Cylinder as political propaganda despite its reputation as the earliest known human rights decree, and even though ten out of eleven textbooks called Cyrus a savior or Messiah. Although all of the surveyed textbooks noted that Athenian democracy benefited a small percentage of the population and promoted slavery and elitism while the Persian Empire provided an admirable stability in fostering a tolerant and relatively peaceful administration, none expanded on this significant difference with respect to human rights as a Western trait. None of the surveyed textbooks demonstrated the treatment of minorities in subsequent Iranian governments such as the Parthian Empire (247 BCE-224 CE) to show which system served the notion of human rights. None of the surveyed textbooks attributed the Code of Chivalry that dominated ancient and medieval Europe to Iranian origins.

This study found that despite majority of the surveyed textbooks crediting the Greco-Persian Wars with the rise of Classical Greece and strengthening of Athenian democracy, none of the textbooks covered Iranian debates about different types of government including democracy prior to the birth of Athenian democracy or the Iranian government's re-installment of democracies in Ionian Greek city-states. This omission does not provide important information to students in analyzing ancient Iranian views as to why they chose monarchy over democracy or oligarchy as a form of government before the establishment of democracy in Athens. Even more importantly, with the surveyed textbooks' omission of how Iranian kings allowed Asiatic Greek city-states under their domain to have democracies, students do not learn that Iranian imperial governance was unique in its tolerance, openness, and inclusivity.

This study demonstrated that although majority of the surveyed textbooks covered the teachings of Zoroastrianism about free will and individual choices along with moral and ethical dualism—with some textbooks labeling these ideas as new and unique—Zoroastrian positioning in the development of individualism, as a Western trait, was vague and incoherent. None of the textbooks in the study connected the concept of individualism in Arthurian legends to Iranian origins. As far as heroism of Iranian sun god Mithras and its adoption by the Romans, only one surveyed textbook discussed such a connection.

Finally, this study discovered that the surveyed textbooks' coverage of the roles of Iranian religions such as Zoroastrianism, Mithraism, and Manichaeism and European Iranians such as the Scythians and Alans in relation to Christianity was lacking, marginalized, incomplete, or incoherent. Six out of eleven textbooks in the study specifically noted Zoroastrian influences on Christianity. As an example of abortive historical teachings, these surveyed textbooks did not expand upon these influences as the subject matter developed. Iranian positioning with respect to the concept and origins of monotheism and ethical dualism were also incomplete and incoherent. For example, if surveyed textbooks claimed that monotheism originated in 14th century BCE Egypt, then they should also note royal marriages between the Egyptian pharaoh Akhenaten and Asiatic princesses of Indo-Iranian Mitanni kingdom given Mithraism (Kak, 2005). Bearing this in mind, the least likely date of sixth century BCE for Zoroaster as proposed by majority of surveyed textbooks marginalized Iranian positioning with respect to monotheism, an important idea that shaped the West. Only a few textbooks in the study referred to Iranian religions of Mithraism or Manichaeism, respectively, as having an impact on Christianity. Only a few surveyed textbooks mentioned the three Magi who visited baby Jesus, but none identified them as Iranian Zoroastrian wisemen. None of the surveyed textbooks discussed the role of Iranian beliefs and the influential early Christian theologians such as St. Ambrose and St. Thomas. None of the textbooks in the study covered the role of European

Iranians such as the Alans and Scythians with respect to spread and development of Christianity in ancient Europe. None of the surveyed textbooks discussed the Holy Grail and its Iranian origins or any relationship between the Vatican and Mithraism.

Implications

As a history educator, the researcher made the following assumptions about this study. First, historians are supposed to tell the truth about what happened in the past. Dunn's (2013) suggestion underpinned this assumption asserting that as soon as a historian has another goal besides discovering and relaying what happened then a historical account is contaminated. Second, textbooks are key tools in higher education. Kornblith and Lasser (2005) and Jaschik (2005) reinforced this assumption in that textbooks reach a much wider audience and shape how college students encounter history. Many educators rely solely on textbooks to design class curriculum and lesson plans (Kornblith & Lasser, 2005). Therefore, content matters. Third, historians, well versed in the field, write and revise college history textbooks. Kornblith and Lasser's (2005) report supported this assumption in that authors, not editors or marketing personnel, control the content of textbooks although only a handful of publishers produce the majority of college textbooks.

Although mainstream approach to teaching Western Civilization history includes the Judeo-Christian-Greco-Roman narrative (Parcel & Taylor, 2015; Arnn, 2014, p. 1; Le Gates, 2001, p. 19; p. 6; Papper, 1995, p. 131), Mohammad (2013) claimed the justification for studying history is to understand the totality of human experiences through factual analysis and approach the discipline holistically. Further, critical pedagogy is important in transformational leadership in education. Therefore, understanding how Iran is positioned in Western Civilization history follows Salinas, Blevins, and Sullivan's (2012) view on critical historical thinking in that not only should historians examine the past through primary sources but include the marginalized or omitted histories—controversial histories—so that formation of an identity is more meaningful (pp. 19-20). Bruno-Jofré and Schiralli (2002) named content knowledge and mastery of the subject matter as part of critical pedagogy for history educators (p. 121), and claimed teaching history should not rest on ulterior political goals (p. 123). Finally, given the current debates about replacing Western Civilization history as a limited perspective glorifying imperialism and colonialism with World history given its broader nature (Ricketts et al., 2011), a thorough coverage of Iran in the origins of Western Civilization may address that curriculum dilemma.

Although experts and textbook authors may debate the extent to which the positioning of Iran and Iranians fits in the origins of Western Civilization, this study revealed that the surveyed college history textbooks covered virtually nothing on the subject matter. The surveyed textbooks are silent on Iran and the origins of the West. According to Taleb (2007), "*what you don't know* [emphasis added]" is "far more relevant than what you do know" (p. 3), because there are so many things one can do with what one does not know. However, people tend to focus too much on what they do know (Taleb, 2007). Based on the results of this study, the researcher proposes a paradigm shift in the teaching of Western Civilization history. The researcher suggests that instead of the limited and incomplete Judeo-Christian-Greco-Roman narrative currently presented (Parcel & Taylor, 2015; Arnn, 2014; Le Gates, 2001; Papper, 1995), the academia consider the *Zoroastrian*-Judeo-Christian and *Iranian*-Greco-Roman traditions in the origins of Western Civilization.

This paradigm shift will transform the perspective of historians in teaching the history of the West and placing Iran and Iranians in that paradigm rather than pushing limited, faulty narrative leading to the results seen in the literature review and the findings of this study. This paradigm shift will transform the knowledge of the educators and educational institutions by increasing their knowledge base so they may present and convey history of the West more accurately. This paradigm shift will transform the quality and accuracy of what writers and publishers print for textbook content that plays a major role in teaching the public. This paradigm shift will transform student learning by providing them with a more holistic and honest perspective while demonstrating common ancestry in enhancing their worldview and cultural relations. This paradigm shift will transform how Westerners access a part of their heritage that textbooks omit or marginalize. This paradigm shift will transform the current decolonization and inequity experienced by peoples of Iranian stock so that the academia does not treat them as *the other* or insignificant with respect to the origins of the West. This paradigm shift will help both Westerners and peoples of Iranian stock reclaim part of their shared history and heritage.

Recommendations for Action

Given the textbooks in the study are virtually silent about the positioning of Iran and Iranians in the origins of Western Civilization, the researcher recommends that textbook authors and publishers engage experts in the field of Iranian studies in formulating content. Authors should identify and incorporate Iranian elements of Western Civilization in textbooks. Authors should provide complete and proper terminology for Iran, Iranians, and Iranian languages. They should fully discuss Iranian origins and spread across Asia and Europe in the Age of Antiquity. Authors should identify all peoples of Iranian stock as Iranian. Authors should discuss and explain Iranian elements in the development of Western traits.

In demonstrating this change, the researcher provides the following examples. Alexander the Great's father Philip II "built his power and created many institutions to imitate those known from the Achaemenid [Persian] Empire" (Olbrycht, 2010, p. 345), because "the most immediate model of a great monarchy was Persia (Olbrycht, 2010, p. 346). Although Alexander later conquered the Achaemenid Persian Empire, he and his court went through Iranization (Olbrycht, 2010, pp. 358 and 355) making "Iranians the mainstay of his army" (Olbrycht, 2010, p. 342). Alexander's Indian War (327-325 BCE) "should be seen as a Macedonian-Iranian victory" given Alexander's army were mostly Iranian (Olbrycht, 2010, p. 360). The surveyed textbooks do not cover the positioning of Iran and Iranians in the history of Hellenistic period. According to Sekunda (2010), Alexander's father Philip adopted the wedge military formation from Iranian Scythians (p. 451). Habashi (2000) explained that the origins of the four elements—air, water, earth, and fire—as mentioned by Greek philosophers are Iranian (p. 115). Littleton and Malcor (2000) claimed that "the steppe Iranians had an enormous influence on Europe" so that at the dawn of the Middle Ages, the Europeans transformed from a Roman-look to an Iranian Sarmatian- or Alanic-look (p. xvii). These examples are only a tip of the iceberg in demonstrating the major implications for a paradigm shift if authors and publishers engage experts in Iranian studies when writing textbooks on Western Civilization history.

In order to disseminate the results of this study, the researcher proposes reaching out to publishers and educational institutions to address deficient content. The researcher recommends meeting with educators, administrators, and writers in sharing these findings and discussing their implications. The researcher recommends producing educational videos to supplement current teaching materials so that educators may address content deficiencies while awaiting textbooks with updated and inclusive materials.

A caveat for engaging those in the field of Iranian studies when writing Western Civilization history textbooks involves making a distinction between a *native* Iran and *post-Islamic* invasion and colonization of Iran in early Middle Ages (7th century onwards). That is, in the Age of Antiquity, Iran was under an Iranian governance and ancestral beliefs such as Zoroastrianism and Mithraism. This distinction is imperative so that Iran's native or ancestral role and identity remain intact without being confused with a foreign ideology known as Islam.

Recommendations for Further Study

This study focused on certain preliminary themes as far as definitions of terms and origins of peoples as well as some traits attributed to the West. Given the breadth of the subject matter, the researcher recommends breaking down each aspect into separate studies. For example, Russell (1992) was disappointed with Yamauchi's (1990/1996) attempt to cover Persia and the Bible, a long overdue subject that should include the latest evidence in formulating a promising and thoughtful coverage (p. 256). Russell (1992) criticized other scholars in their lack of depth and failure to note "extraordinary important" imagery in Iranian religion (p. 258). He stressed there is a "need for a balanced assessment" with respect to Iran's role in Judaism and Christianity (p. 258). On Yamauchi (1990/1996), Russell (1992) added, "there is no proper focus on religious questions, nor are they developed in a chronological context" (p. 259). Therefore, a future study may focus strictly on Iran's positioning with respect to Christianity.

A future study may focus on Iranian elements in Greco-Roman laws and intellectualism such as Greek Medism, Aristotle's concept of arête versus Iranian idea of arta, and Plutarch on Persian king Artaxerxes. A study may involve the coverage of Indo-Europeans and the Indo-European Iranian branch as key components of origins of Western Civilization (Samiei, 2014). The omission or marginalization of the positioning of Iran and Iranians with respect to Indo-European history might be attributing to public misconceptions about categorization of *white* people. In a recent report, students at SOAS University of London were calling for removal of white philosophers from curriculum to address diversity (Pasha-Robinson, 2017). Even the word

Caucasian for white people may be Iranian in origin. According to the Roman author Pliny the Elder, the name of the Caucasus Mountains comes from the Iranian Scythian word *Graucasus* meaning white with snow (Pliny the Elder, trans. 1847, p. 116).

Additional studies should focus on European Iranians and the origins of the West so that authors incorporate them in textbooks about the history of Western Civilization. For example, the 2004 movie *King Arthur* presented the *Sarmatian Theory*—a theory that proposes the Arthurian tales arose from "a Roman officer named Lucius Artorius Castus, the commander of a group of warriors from a nomadic tribe known as the Sarmatians" (Matthews, 2004, p. 112). However, neither the 2004 movie nor Matthews (2004) identified Sarmatians as Iranians. Throughout the movie, the Sarmatian knights and, ultimately their leader Arthur, shouted the battle cry *Rus!*—something that created a buzz among viewers on the Internet as to its meaning. Russian-American historian George Vernadsky claimed that Rus derived from the name of the Iranian Alanic tribe known as Rukhs (Roxolani or Roxalani) meaning the radiant, and that the name of Russia presumably derived from Rus (Vernadsky, 1969, p. 22; as cited by Riasanovsky & Steinberg, 2011, p. 22). In looking at Roman emperors, Maximinis Thrax (173-238)—and others with similar ethnicity—is of interest given his father was of Germanic Goths while his mother of Iranian Alans (Pearson, 2016, p. 1).

Future studies do not have to be restricted to the Age of Antiquity. Researchers may look for Iranian footprints in modern history of Western Civilization. For example, a study may focus on Zoroastrianism and the modern West. In a letter to the president of then Yale College Ezra Stiles, American Founding Father and polymath Benjamin Franklin wrote about the recent translation of Zoroaster's writings called Zend-Avesta and said he would ship Stiles a copy given its teachings of morality (Franklin, 1772). French composer and music theorist Rameau's revolutionary and avant-garde opera *Zoroastre* (1749) took place in an imaginary Persia and dealt with Zoroastrian cosmic duality philosophy of good versus evil. French author and intelligence officer Andre Robert de Nerciat wrote an eclectic and mystical piece entitled *Zoroaster's Telescope* (1796). In Victor Hugo's *The Hunchback of Notre-Dame* (1831), the Archdeacon of Notre Dame said, "Zoroaster taught the same! the sun is born of fire, the moon of the sun. Fire is the soul of the Great All" (Hugo, 1888, p. 48). Of course, there is German philosopher Friedrich Nietzsche's *Thus Spoke Zarathustra* (1885) considered his most significant work in the field of philosophy (Wicks, 2016). In an article by *The Nation* (America's oldest continuously published weekly journal), Zoroaster is referred to as "the great Persian legislator" ("The Week," 1871, p. 315) and praised for his teachings that planting trees is one of the most admirable acts. Apparently, Mozart loved riddles and one night during the 1786 Viennese carnival, he went to a masquerade party dressed as an Eastern philosopher passing out handwritten riddles and proverbs entitled "Excerpts from the Fragments of Zoroaster" (Wood, 2003, p. 26). In the United States, one finds Zoroaster's marble statue by Edward Potter (1857-1923) at New York Appellate Court House, Zoroaster's statue at the Rockefeller Memorial Chapel at the University of Chicago, and a peak at the Grand Canyon in Arizona called the Zoroaster Temple.

    The researcher proposes that decolonization of Iran's positioning in history is dichotomous in nature. First, as discussed earlier, further studies should take place on Iran's positioning in the origins of Western Civilization. Second, new studies should begin on Iran's positioning in world history post Islamic invasion and occupation of its lands in early Middle Ages onwards given Iranian attributes are misappropriated to non-Iranians such as Arabs or Muslims (Kincheloe, 2004; Anvarinejad, 2007; Foltz, 2016; Shariati, 2010), seen under the prism of Orientalism (Daryaee, 2005), or left out in favor of non-Iranians such as Turks or Arabs (Brockway, 2007; Morgan, 2008; Morgan & Walker, 2008) leading to further inequity for Iranians in the field of history. A potential study under this perspective involves Iranian languages. The researcher has noted a recent trend in some referring to Persian, one of many Iranian languages, as Farsi. Suren-Pahlavi (2007) also addressed this phenomenon. The study of this trend is timely and imperative as it falls under historical misconceptions. As demonstrated in this study, Persia/Persian is a proxy for Iran/Iranian, not Farsi. It is erroneous to begin calling the historical Persian language Farsi just as one does not refer to Farsi carpet, Farsi cat, Farsi rose, Farsi food, Farsi history, or anything else that is Iranian (Persian). Additionally, Farsi is the Arabized version of the Iranian word Persian. Therefore, by using Farsi rather than historical Persian, Iranians are facing continued marginalization and colonization.

Conclusion

History is about meaning making and learning about one's roots and identity. According to the American Historical Association, historians should be involved in critical dialogue and respecting the integrity of historical records. They should ensure that sources do not alter, suppress, or change evidence (American Historical Association, 2011, p. 3). They should present different perspectives about historical events since "absolute historical knowledge is denied us" (American Historical Association, 2011, p. 5). Historians should acknowledge personal biases affecting, and financial support from special interest groups influencing, scholarly work. Good teaching involves accuracy and rigor in transmitting information. Textbooks and teaching materials should include "the diversity of human experience, recognizing that historical accuracy requires attention both to individual and cultural similarities and differences and to the larger global and historical context within which societies have evolved" (American Historical Association, 2011, p. 9).

Critical pedagogy is important in transformational leadership in education. Educators are obligated to point out errors or problems in content and mainstream narratives. In regards to teaching history of Western Civilization, one should recall the warnings of its looming demotion by Ricketts et al. (2011) because unfortunately teaching it "had come to be seen as a form of apologetics for racism, imperialism, sexism, and colonialism" (p. 14). It appears that in perceiving that something is missing from or fragmented in Western Civilization history content, educational institutions are now marginalizing and omitting it from their curriculum in America, a Western nation. Therefore, the significance of this study is the need for authors and educators to shift the currently flawed narrative on the history of the West. Iran's positioning is a key component in the study of Western Civilization. The researcher argues that Iran and Iranians not only influenced the making of the West; they are part of the West. By placing Iran and Iranians where they belong, historians may also address concerns about teaching the history of the West (Ricketts et al., 2011).

www.ingramcontent.com/pod-product-compliance
Lightning Source LLC
LaVergne TN
LVHW011959070526
838202LV00054B/4963